PATHWAY TO PURPOSE

Women Answer God's Call to Leadership

A Workbook

by

Kathrine Giske

Kharis Enterprises Publishing

A Division of Kharis Enterprises Pty Ltd ABN: 61 831 018 044
8 Parkdale Court Robina Queensland Australia 4226
Phone: +61 7 55 930 360 Fax: +61 7 55 930 084
E-mail: kharis@usa.com

Cover: Lee Sattler & Kharis Enterprises Pty Ltd
Editorial/Production: Victropolis Creative Services (www.victropolis.com)
Publishers: Kharis Enterprises Pty Ltd (kharis@usa.com)

Unless otherwise noted, all scriptures were taken from the New American Standard Bible, © 1960, 1963, 1968, 1971, 1972, 1973, 1975, 1977 by The Lockman Foundation. Used by permission.

Printed in Australia

ISBN 0 9578329 0 7

But the path of the righteous is like the light of dawn.

That shines brighter and brighter until the full day.

—Proverbs 4:18

In memory of my mother, Helen,
who inspired me to follow God's purpose
at all cost.

ACKNOWLEDGEMENTS

- To the board members of Women's Leadership Network, Ginny Randolph, Dee Brown, Lee Sattler, and Betty Hart for their encouragement, prayers, and input. It was their idea that this book should be written. May the Lord use its message to challenge many women to find God's purpose.

- To my dear friend Lee Sattler for providing valuable insights, developing the book's title, and providing the cover design.

- To Meg Crossman for her labor of love to meticulously review and edit the first draft, and for her challenge to keep refining its message.

- To Tina Viney, who provided excellent input as a professional woman, mother, and sister. She believes in the message of this book.

- To my other reviewers, Dr. Iverna Tompkins, Dr. Miriam Adeney, and Dr. Dellanna O'Brien, for their endorsements of this book and their valuable input to the author.

- To Vic Lipsey, the editor, who suffered through the drafts, and whose careful reading of the text resulted in a much better book than would otherwise have been possible.

- Finally, a deep appreciation to my husband, Steve, for graciously accommodating the long days and nights needed to complete the writing of this book. Your support and encouragement were important.

CONTENTS

Women are complex creatures. Think about it:

- At 20 we want to be *beautiful*.
- At 30 we want to be married and start a *family*.
- At 40 we want to be *successful*.
- At 50 we want to be *rich*.
- At 60 we want to be *respected*.
- At 70 we want to be *healthy*.
- At 80 we just want to *wake up*.
- At the end of our life we want to be *remembered*!

I had just completed a women's retreat. A few days later the organizers asked to have lunch with me to solicit my input on the event. Halfway into our conversation one of the women remarked, "Our retreats are always well attended. The programs and the speakers are great, but we seem to struggle in one area. We want to recruit leaders. Somehow we fail to attract them. What can we do to solve this dilemma?"

"It's quite simple," I answered. "To attract leaders you have to develop a program that appeals to *leaders*."

As our discussion on women and leadership continued we realized that there are few opportunities for women to be mentored for leadership by other women. Perhaps it's because women are ambivalent about this subject in the first place. After all, how many women do you know who aspire to become chief executive officers of corporations, or generals in the military, or even pastors of local churches? Married women expect their husbands to provide leadership in the home—or at least hope for it. With those perceptions, it's easy to understand why many women dismiss the function of leadership as irrelevant.

However, that's not the end of the story. Our conversation also explored the idea that women all over the world long to *feel* deeply, to *think* creatively, and to *enjoy* the fruit of their labor. They long to find God's heart and calling for their lives. Many women believe God has given them a vision to do something important. What they lack is an understanding of God's ways in leadership. If only they could find a mature woman to mentor them, the possibilities would be endless.

By the time our lunch meeting was over, we sensed the Lord tugging at our hearts to develop an organization to train women leaders. God sovereignly led a group of women to develop the Women's Leadership Network. Since its inception in 1995, WLN has trained many women to answer God's call to leadership. Its advisory board is comprised of prominent senior pastors who provide spiritual accountability and strongly endorse its programs. National and international interest in WLN is expanding quickly because Christian women hunger to learn how to be purposeful.

Pathway to Purpose introduces you to the eight exciting disciplines women from all walks of life are learning from WLN's program. It will help you develop the disciplines you need to lead an intentional, purposeful life. You can simply read the book for enjoyment and information. Or you can use it as a study guide for powerful, personal growth. Or you can study the book with a mentor or in a small group. Since there are eight chapters in the book, you may want to dedicate eight weeks to review and discuss the material. At the end of each chapter are suggestions to help you develop your personal strategy for that discipline. If you take the time to reflect on the questions and complete the exercises, you will be surprised at what you learn about yourself.

One way to assess your personal growth is to fill in the self-assessment questionnaire *before* reading the book. Then when you've completed the program, review your questionnaire answers and see how you have changed.

Leadership Is Influence!

I am surprised to find the Bible has very little to say about leadership except by example. Rather the Bible talks about the qualities that *all* Christians should have. "Love your neighbor (which includes your leaders, your peers and your subordinates) as you love yourself. So the biblical idea is much closer to the way women think and act than do men.[1]

As you ponder this issue, perhaps you are wondering, "I'm not sure if I *am* a leader?" Please read on before you settle on that issue.

Ask a dozen people to define *leadership* and you'll probably receive a dozen different answers. That's because *leadership* is an elusive term. It means different things to different people. Most people equate leadership with management. In fact, most leadership books are about management.

Leadership requires management skills to be effective, but it doesn't stop there. It's more. I have to agree with John Maxwell's definition. "Leadership is *influence.* That's it. Nothing more; nothing less. He who thinks he leadeth and hath no one following is only taking a walk. Leadership is the ability to obtain followers."[2]

If we define leadership as *influence*, it takes on a whole new meaning and relevance for *women*. It is my conviction that every woman is called to lead because she has been given platforms of influence—in the home, the workplace, her church, the community, and in society at large. When women recognize this God-given gift, they become important instruments in God's hands to carry out His purposes. This being true, it follows that practically every woman can be a leader at some point in her life. In most cases however, it is only when we look back on a situation that we can say, "That person was the leader", or to use John Maxwell's term, "That person had an influence on *people* which affected the outcome."

Remember Esther? She recognized the moment of her destiny and exercised her influence to save the Jewish people from Haman's evil plan of total extinction.

Consider the late Princess Diana? She never worked for her favorite charities, but she used her influence to raise enormous support and funds for them. She captured the public's attention for important causes.

Mothers can exercise a leadership role to influence and help shape their children's character and values. Today many women use *open parenting*—the delegation of responsibility to children to make their own decisions. What they don't understand is that *someone* will influence their children; if the parents don't do it, the children will seek out and find it elsewhere. It's a matter of whether or not the parent wants to be a part of that process.

Teachers don't usually manage people, but their ideas and thoughts can influence their students to one day become tomorrow's leaders.

Women who work in the corporate world can influence those around them, including their supervisors, through their life and witness. Even if they do not become the company's CEO, their experience may lead them to start their own business. Why not? Thousands of women today are becoming successful entrepreneurs.

Women who serve in a ministry capacity can influence people in their spiritual development. This has eternal value and will be richly rewarded by the Lord.

Are you convinced now that you are a leader? Consider this: The purpose of leadership is the *pursuit* of God. It involves lifting your head to look at His horizon, not your own. It involves asking the question, "Lord, for what purpose have you uniquely designed me?"

The answer will not come from the systems of this world. Nor from well-meaning friends. The answer will come only as you sit at God's feet and allow Him to work in your life. It is your pathway to God's heart. It is your pathway to purpose. This book was designed to help *you* in that journey.

Finding Your Life's Purpose
Self-Assessment Questionnaire

Take a few minutes to complete this questionnaire. When you have completed all of the exercises in the entire book, answer these questions again. Do you see any changes that have come from what you have learned?

Vision and Goals

a) Do you have an area of special interest or passion? Where did it come from and how did it develop?

b) What are your goals and priorities for this year?

c) Has God given you a promise or a dream that is yet to be fulfilled? What do you think is hindering its fulfillment?

Core Values

a) What are your three most important values?

b) If you had a motto for your life, what would it be?

c) Describe a person who has greatly inspired your life. What qualities do you admire most about that person?

Profile

a) What are your greatest strengths?

b) What is your greatest shortcoming? How would your life improve by overcoming it?

c) What is the most important insight you gained about yourself in the past year?

d) Describe yourself in one word. Is that the way you want to be known?

e) What motivates you personally, professionally, spiritually?

Personal Development

a) Where have you served as a leader in the past and where are you serving now?

b) Where would you like to improve in the leadership roles you already play?

c) Do you know someone who could mentor you in one of these areas?

Chapter One

♦ ♦ ♦

The Power of a Dream

Apprehend God's Purpose and Vision for Your Life

The center of power is not to be found in summit meetings or in peace conferences. It is not in Peking or Washington or the United States, but rather where a child of God prays in the power of the Spirit for God's will to be done in her life, in her home, and in the world about her.

—Ruth Bell Graham

The Power of a Dream
Apprehend God's Purpose and Vision for Your Life

"Lord, teach me to listen. The times are noisy and my ears weary with the thousand raucous sounds which continuously assault them. Give me the spirit of Samuel when he said to You, "Speak, for Thy servant heareth." Let me hear You speaking in my heart. Let me get used to the sound of Your voice, that its tones may be familiar when the sounds of this earth die and the only sound will be the music of Your speaking voice. Amen."

—A. W. Tozer

Commentary

Shira could have had anything she wanted. She was attractive, intelligent, and very popular. Her parents aspired to see her work alongside them in their highly successful ministry. But Shira had a different vision: a deep love for the Jewish people. Israel was to become her home and her land of citizenship. It was a vision with many risks and no guarantees, but it was God's call for this talented woman. Today Shira and her Israeli husband, Ari, and their two children live in Tel Aviv, where they lead an effective ministry training Jewish believers in the ways of God. Shira dared to pursue her dream. What gives a woman the courage to do that? What kinds of things can hold you back?

The Power of a Dream

Everything that exists today started with a dream. And the ability to dream is a God-given gift. It's a reflection of being made in His image. You have been given a divine destiny, a special role to play in humanity's rich tapestry "for such a time as this."

Like Shira, you are called to serve uniquely in your time and your generation. If you are married, begin by honoring your high calling of wife and mother. The home is often the place where many leadership principles are developed. As you are obedient in this call, keep your heart and mind open to God's horizon. His purpose for your life may include something beyond your present vision. It did for me.

Like most women, I dreamt of finding a loving husband and raising a family. God had a different plan. It involved postponing marriage for many years to serve Him as a single woman. For almost ten years I lived out of a suitcase, traveling and working in over fifty countries as a missions leader. The road was not always easy. In time, I learned to focus on the *Lord's* purpose rather than my circumstances.

A Story from My Travel Journal

During one trip to Central Asia I discovered that my passport, two airline tickets, and all my cash were stolen. I was stranded in a remote Muslim nation called Turkmenistan, which borders Iran. The American embassy personnel assured me I could safely return to the US with just their official explanation letter.

When I arrived in London to board the last connecting flight to the US, everything came to a halt. British Airways was not satisfied with the wording in the embassy's letter. They categorically refused to let me board their plane. To obtain passport verification, I needed to travel an hour and a half to the American embassy in downtown London. Unfortunately, it was Saturday and the embassy was closed until the following Tuesday. What was I to do?

Exhausted after three weeks of travel in Central Asia and now stranded in England with no money, I did the female thing: I cried for half an hour. Strangely, nothing happened. No angels appeared. No prince showed up to rescue me. No sympathy came from strangers. It was not a catastrophe, but emotionally it felt like one.

Then I remembered the Lord's call and vision. It gave me the courage to stand up and face my circumstances with full knowledge that God was in control. Over the next five days I found housing, located the embassy, and secured a new visa—all without any cash! When I needed four English pounds for a passport photo, a total stranger came up and, without saying a word, gave me the exact change. How did he know I needed that money? I wonder!

A leader without a vision is like a boat without an anchor. You will drift with the wind if nothing is holding you down. Knowing God's purpose and vision empowers you to face life's challenges *without* intimidation. It helps you to decide on your priorities so you can live your life purposefully. It gives you a sense of direction so you can take others with you. During my extended stay in London the Lord graciously met my needs. In turn, He gave me an opportunity to be His witness to several people who inquired about my situation. God has a way of working things out when you trust Him.

How a Vision Is Discovered

Finding God's purpose and vision requires that you look to see where God is at work as well as the present context or situation which impacts your life. A vision is about something that can be better, different. The process is something like this:

What is the (my) world like?
|
What does the Bible say it should be like?
|
What needs to happen to make it the way God says it should be?
|
What's my role in that?
|
How can I involve others?

Vision is the ability to discern God's plan or purpose behind your present circumstances. If you only attempt things you have already mastered you stop growing. A vision will often stretch you beyond your comfort zone. Your steps of obedience will make the process a rich experience that has merit all by itself. Here are some ways vision is discovered:

The Burning-Bush Experience
The burning bush took Moses by surprise. For forty years he happily pastured his father-in-law's flocks, and then he encountered God on the mountain. There, on holy ground, Moses received God's call to return to Egypt and lead the children of

Israel back to the Promised Land. The call was clear and direct. At first Moses did not feel qualified for the task. God reminded him that he was holding a shepherd's staff. When used according to God's instructions it would become transformed into a powerful tool to help him do the job.

The burning-bush experience is when God *distinctly* speaks to you about His purpose for your life. It can come during a time of prayer, as you encounter a need, or through a word from someone you respect. Here is how one couple received their call.

John was a professional athlete. One summer, his team played in Guatemala. At the end of the game a crowd of children rushed up to meet him. John was accustomed to signing autographs for his fans and was prepared with pen in hand. This time it was different. The children were not interested in his signature. They wanted money so they could have food to eat. As John relayed the experience to his wife they both wept. Their extreme wealth looked like an insult against the backdrop of poverty those children endured. That's when God spoke to both their hearts to do something about it. They returned to the US and established a foundation to provide funds to feed, care for and educate the children of Guatemala.

That's a burning-bush experience. Let's remember though that burning-bush experiences come in all sizes and speeds. God can put on your heart to do something in a small situation and to do it now. We see a need. We use the tool God has put in our hands. We recruit others. That's how the journey begins.

The Emmaus Road Experience
They were seven miles from Jerusalem and these two men had a lot to talk about. The events of the past few days had been staggering. In the midst of their intense conversation someone joined them on their journey. Only some time into the conversation did they recognize He was Jesus.

The Emmaus Road experience is when God's call is revealed *gradually* to you while you are on a journey. You will look back and realize that God was leading you all along. Mother Theresa received her call that way.

A Catholic nun of Albanian ethnicity, Mother Theresa understood poverty. Her family and her people struggled to make ends meet. When she witnessed the degradation of human life on the streets of Calcutta, she responded with Christian compassion. She decided the responsible and Christ-like thing to do was to start the order of the Sisters of Charity and care for the poorest of the poor. But God's purpose was to elevate Mother Theresa to become an ambassador for the poor. Her message would be broadcast to millions everywhere, challenging them to shoulder their responsibility to care, feed, and come alongside the poor in their cities. Today, her order serves in over forty countries. In 1995 the international community awarded her the Nobel Peace Prize. Mother Theresa's call came as an Emmaus Road experience.

The Widow's-Mite Experience

The Pharisees were known for flaunting their religious practices. Jesus wanted His disciples to live by a different standard. Calling their attention to a widow one day, he said, "this poor widow put in more than all the contributors to the treasury. They all put in out of their surplus, but she out of her poverty, put in all she owned, all she had to live on" (Mark 12:43).

That was a humble woman seeking to live her life faithfully before the Lord. She was not interested in drawing attention to herself. Yet her simple act of obedience caught Jesus' watchful eye. She gave Him all she had, and her generosity did not go unnoticed. Many generations later, she is still remembered for that act of obedience.

The author C. S. Lewis had a widow's-mite experience. His relatively short life was devoted to giving lectures and writing essays and commentaries on the Christian faith. While he lived, Lewis' intellectual peers did not fully appreciate his work. It was not until after his death that his work became recognized as a classic in Christian literature. Lewis had no idea that his life and work would have an impact on future generations.

A widow's-mite experience is the motivation to live your life in *obedience* to the Lord whether the world considers you a success or not. It is being faithful in what God has given you, however little that might be, and trusting that He will reward you in due course.

Where Are You in Your Journey?

Making time to seek God's vision may seem like a luxury you can't afford. For example, if you are a mother with a young family, you may be thinking, *Take time to dream? Lady, you've got to be kidding!* Yes, parenting is demanding. So recognize that God is working His purposes in you every day, even in the midst of a hectic schedule. Your subconscious mind is like an invisible cooker, where your ideas simmer while you are busy doing other things. (Most creative minds operate that way. Galileo, Newton, and others made important discoveries while busy with unrelated activities.) The first step is joyfully embracing the responsibilities you carry now.

And stay open to the Lord and allow Him to plant seeds in your heart that may blossom in later years. It may be an interest in a special need or a language. You may take up a small role of service that develops an expertise as you practice it. It is our choices that show what we truly are, far more than our abilities.

Recognize Life's Distractions

It is a documented fact that the most talented, creative and capable people frequently fall prey to burnout. Perhaps it's because their competence finds many avenues of expression. People constantly seek their assistance and counsel. Soon schedules get full, days grow long and time for reflection and rest become scarce. That's how burnout begins.

The only way to remain true to God's call and purpose is to diligently guard your quiet times and faithfully schedule them into each day. They say that without darkness there are no dreams. Every God inspired vision will come under attack either from forces within you (fear and doubt) or through people or circumstances that appear to undermine the integrity of the vision. That's why it's important to recognize and identify others who share the same vision. *Accomplishing* your vision will always involve other people. Meanwhile, don't be discouraged or distracted when you face challenges. They may look like this:

1. People May Not Understand Your Vision

When Joseph shared his dream with his brothers, they scoffed at him and sold him into slavery. It would have been natural to doubt the vision at that point. Instead, Joseph refused to doubt God. He kept the vision deep in his heart until its fulfillment.

2. People May Want You to Change the Vision

When God gives you a vision, He expects you to carry it out, not change it. When a pastor I know tried to introduce his church to a new vision, the membership dropped from 4,000 to almost 800. The new vision did not have the foundation it needed. It almost destroyed the church. Today, this church is vibrant again and has a new pastor who is honoring the mandate of the original vision.

Don't shortcut or change your vision. You may be disappointed with the results.

3. You May Not Fully Understand the Vision

Sometimes the Lord does not give you the full picture. He may give you one piece and expect you to walk in it before revealing the next step. It may unfold in a different way than you envisioned. Stay true to what He has given, and don't rush ahead on your own.

Moses was a man of God. However, because he disobeyed and struck the rock twice with his rod, the Lord did not allow him to enter the Promised Land (see Num. 20:12).

4. People May Question Your Call to Leadership

Women whose leadership gifts are developing but who are sensing God's call to step out often experience this resistance from friends and family. Someone may say, "What *qualifies* you to be a leader?"

There will always be *someone* who does that, often because they will never follow *you* (because of chemistry, different vision, lack of trust, or lack of understanding of your calling etc.) You may want to try to *convert* them, but if you fail just smile and move on.

5. Guard Against Your Need to Be Needed

Women are nurturers by nature. There is a certain joy in knowing that you have eased someone's pain or comforted them in their hour of need. Even the late Princess Diana used her humanitarian work to not only bless others, but also to receive personal validation.

Yet in the act of compassion, in the giving of comfort, women need to guard against the temptation of prolonged involvement out of a need to be needed. This is one strategy the enemy uses to involve you in relationships that extend far beyond God's intention. This dynamic is sometimes called *codependency*. A woman can develop codependent relationships with her children by becoming too protective and overbearing. She can become codependent with her spouse by compromising truth and honesty in order to please her husband.

The question to ask is "Am I focused on God's vision, or am I using my work as a means for personal validation?"

6. Guard Against the Retirement Syndrome

Don't let your age be an excuse for not pursuing God's vision. Fifty is a critical age for many women. It's a time when the demands of raising a family have diminished. Suddenly there is more free time than before. It can be a crossroads. You can either put to good use a lifetime of wisdom, or escape into early retirement.

This is an important time for women to step out and make a difference with their lives. I think of women like Katherine Graham, Mary Kay, and Margaret Thatcher. Their stories begin with what others may regard as a conclusion. Rather than retire into oblivion, they used this season of their lives to launch new dreams. They turned this season into their finest hours.

The question to ask is "To what great need does the Lord want me to apply my greatest passion?"

Find Your Part in Accomplishing the Vision

Vision is the indispensable quality of leadership. A leader with a vision and the ability to communicate it effectively will soon attract others who share the same vision or want to serve that vision. Sometimes your vision is to play a part in someone else's vision. Sometimes others have already realized your vision and your call is to join them. Consider the following steps as you evaluate your part in accomplishing the vision.

1. The Best Lessons in Leadership Are Learned by Observing Others
Leadership is about influencing *people.* You learn it by observing other's responses to you and your responses to them. Today many organizations are using the "360 degree evaluation." Each person's superior, peers and subordinates are asked to evaluate the person's performance. *Leaders need to be evaluated too!*

2. Know What God Expects of You
I know some women who believe God has given them a great vision but do nothing to move in that direction. They expect God to do it all. As a result, they wonder why it's taking the Lord so long to make it happen.

It's *your* responsibility to know God's desire and to do what He expects of you. As you exercise your faith and take initiative based on His promises to you, His purposes will be fulfilled. *The miracle begins when you take the first step!*

3. Develop Your Communication Skills
Words are the arsenal of leadership. In the book *The Articulate Executive*, author Grandville Toogood says, "The formula for success is not necessarily all competence. The formula for success is part competence and the rest the ability to articulate that competence—in a way that is not *average* or even *predictable.*"[3]

In a recent letter to me, Dr. Ed Dayton, former Vice-President of World Vision International made this distinction between men and women's communication styles. "It is men who evaluate women as poor communicators because the men are using their influence style on other men. Women take the time to give you the background, give you a feel for where they are coming from. They do this because they want to *influence* you on the basis of interpersonal relationships. Men need a lot more work in this area, and if "servant leadership" is the style we promote, women have it much more than men."[4]

4. Keep a Balanced Pace between You and Your Team
Vision is essential to leadership. However, even a great vision will fail to attract followers if the leader's stride is too far ahead of those who want to follow. Jesus set an excellent example of leadership. He taught the disciples and then sent them out two by two to give them an opportunity to practice. He observed their ability to follow while still keeping His lead. *Balance your pace so others can follow your leadership.*

5. Acquire a Position of Leadership through Encouragement
I remember meeting a friend at a public function. She was a mother of five. When I asked her what she was doing, she answered, "Nothing much. Compared to your life I'm not doing enough." "What do you mean?" I replied. "You are raising five small children. That makes you the CEO of your organization. Think of the leadership skills that you use to carry out your job each day: time management, planning, training, conflict resolution, health and hygiene" She laughed and nodded. "You're right, *I am* doing a lot." *Look for ways to affirm and empower others. It's a leadership prerequisite.*

6. Build Corporate Ownership of a Vision
Sometimes small ideas or steps blossom in a way that far exceeds our expectations. I'm sure when Bill Gates wrote the first operating system for the IBM PC (personal computer) he had no idea that his invention would spawn a brand new industry and launch a technological revolution. When Mrs. Fields baked her first cookie she did not expect her recipes to one day become the product of a multi-million dollar industry. These were ideas whose time had come but their success needed a leader who knew how to *continually communicate the vision* to others so they owned it for themselves. That's when a vision becomes contagious and grows. *If a vision is important it deserves to be owned by others.* Find compelling ways to communicate it so it is passed on.

Celebrate Each Season

Winston Churchill once said, "Leaders can never afford to lose the beauty of life in the corrosive tedium of work." In the process of finding God's purpose and vision, learn to enjoy life's journey and accept the rhythm of each season. Life is dynamic and cyclical. Your values should always stay the same, but your priorities will change. Each season will have a different rhythm. It may look like the following.

A Time to *Retreat*

Jesus regularly went to the mountains to be alone with the Father. In the quiet, away from the demands and noise of the crowds, he talked and communed with His Father. Those private retreats gave Jesus the strength to carry out His earthly mission.

You need those times of quiet too. They will help you remain focused on your priorities. They will allow you to develop intimacy with the Lord and learn from Him. Make time for personal retreats so that God can speak to you.

A Time to *Advance*

The exertion needed to lift a shuttle into outer space is so intense that the astronauts must be strapped to their posts in order to endure it. That's how life feels during times of a personal "lift off." This can be especially true when you enter a new professional field, personal direction, or unfamiliar assignment. Your learning curve is usually steep. Your life might seem out of balance, and you may have little time to rest. Stay focused and keep moving. This is your season to advance.

A Time to *Persevere*

In this season you simply do what you've always done without fanfare or fireworks. You sow the seeds of faithfulness. You walk by faith, not by sight. Perseverance is a key attribute in all achievers, and this season is your time to develop this discipline.

What season are you in right now? Do you know your priorities? Do you feel you are growing as a person?

The vision of a dying world is vast before our eyes.
We feel the heartbeat of its nee, we hear its feeble cries.
Lord Jesus Christ, revive your church in this her crucial hour!
Lord Jesus Christ, awake your church with Spirit given power.

(Macedonia written by Ann Orlund)

Summary

Helen Keller was asked, "What would be worse than being born blind?" She replied, "To have sight without vision."

We can be endowed with the trappings of success—money, a nice house and many friends—but if we lack vision, our life will drift and have little meaning. Happiness lies not in how much you possess, but in how grateful you are for what you have. A vision brings substance to your life. It helps you find joy in everything you do, no matter how small. It opens your eyes to the value of people and the meaning of events.

Are you excited about the possibilities of your vision? Over the past few years Women's Leadership Network has seen many women find God's purpose and vision and develop leadership disciplines. Here are some ways women were impacted. You may be encouraged to see the power of a dream.

- A retired psychiatrist had a lifelong dream of working in China. After completing this program she and her husband were able to see that dream fulfilled. Today they both serve the Lord in China, working with government leaders.
- A businesswoman applied the principles of this course to her business. It became so successful that in one year she was able to pay off her business and home mortgages and become debt free.
- A former mayor was able to develop new spiritual disciplines that prepared her for a long-term career in politics.
- A Microsoft employee resigned from her lucrative position to start an international ministry that trains women in poor countries and provides small business loans to them with the goal of strengthening the church in those countries.
- A hairdresser discovered the gift of intercessory prayer and is now involved in praying for Christian leaders and nations around the world.

In this chapter you have reviewed the following:
- ☐ God's vision will give you the courage to face life's challenges.
- ☐ A leader without vision will soon lose her focus.
- ☐ Even when you aren't aware of your vision, God will work His purposes in your life.
- ☐ You will learn the biggest lessons in leadership on your own.
- ☐ Life is dynamic and cyclical. Priorities will change but your values stay the same.

Building A Strategy for Your Vision

A good strategy is built by asking good questions that focus not on *how* to do something but *why.* Here are some questions to ask yourself as you develop your vision.

- What stirrings have you felt as you've read this chapter on vision?
- What is God saying to you through this challenge?
- What tools or skills has God put in your hands to serve this need?
- What do you believe God expects from you?
- Who will resource you in this vision? How can you partner with others?

Once you've answered these questions and identified goals for personal growth, read on. The following chapters are designed to help you develop new skills for the future.

Read, Reflect, & Respond

The following exercises are designed to help you think *strategically* about your life and your circumstances so you can discover God's purposes in them. These aren't easy questions. They may make you feel uncomfortable. At times you may wonder "Where is this leading to?" Take time to prayerfully ponder these questions. You could gain a new perspective on the way you view yourself, your circumstances and those around you.

Bible Study

Take a few minutes alone to read and reflect on the following Scripture. Record your thoughts in a journal.

PROVERBS 29:18. *Where there is no vision, the people are unrestrained. But happy is he who keeps the law.*
What are some ways you get distracted when you are not focused on your vision or on important priorities?

Homework Question

Take 45 minutes alone with the Lord and write down what you believe is His vision for your life. If you know what it is, use this time to reflect on how the Lord would have you live this out. If you don't have a vision, use this time to wait on Him for direction. Don't dismiss anything He says, no matter how far-fetched it seems.

Small Group Question

What is an area of need God has brought to your attention lately? How do you feel compelled to respond?

Recommended Reading
If you are a group studying this book you may want to assign one or two people to read one of these books and present a book report to the group.

Seven Habits of Highly Effective People, Stephen Covey (Simon and Schusters: New York). Excellent guide for developing a personal mission statement.

THE POWER OF A DREAM

Developing the Leader within You, John C. Maxwell (Thomas Nelson Publishers: Nashville, Tennessee). A recommended companion to this workbook.

The Making of a Leader, Dr. J. Robert Clinton (NavPress: Colorado Springs, Colorado). Provides a detailed guide on how to develop a timeline of important personal milestones.

Read, Reflect & Respond

Chapter Two

◆ ◆ ◆

The Art of Mentoring

Refine Your Purpose through Accountability

My business is not to remake myself, but to make the absolute best of what God made.

—*Robert Browning*

The Art of Mentoring
Refine Your Purpose through Accountability

Lord, help me to find the purpose for which I am uniquely designed. Grant me the courage to change those things that can be changed. Teach me how I can learn from others so in the end of my life's journey I can stand before You and hear You say, 'Well done, good and faithful servant.'

Commentary

My initiation into the world of cooking began with the mundane task of cleaning pots and pans. For the life of me, I couldn't understand how cleaning dishes would prepare me for cooking. But it did.

Mother's plan was to help me understand the rhythm of working in the kitchen. By being there, I learned the secrets behind her delicious recipes and gained the courage to attempt them myself. I learned how to use rosemary and garlic to add aromatic flavor to roasted potatoes. How sauces can be spiced up by using chicken broth as a base. How to make meat moist and tender by marinating it in lemon juice and balsamic vinegar.

Among women, mentoring comes in many forms. In my case, it required I perform mundane tasks in order to learn from an expert. It was time well spent, and the principles I learned have stayed with me ever since.

THE ART OF MENTORING

How Women Mentor Each Other

Throughout history women have mentored and co-mentored each other out of necessity, out of habit, and out of tradition. When Ruth decided to follow Naomi to her homeland, she needed to learn the ways and customs of her mother-in-law's people. Every step of the way, Naomi mentored Ruth on how to conduct herself around Boaz and catch his attention. In the end, Boaz won the girl!

Mentoring among women has been a part of society since the beginning of time, especially in traditional cultures. Most of these relationships happen informally, but not always. Women mentor each other in cooking, in domestic tasks, and in customs and traditions. In Japan mothers mentor their daughters in the Japanese art of gift-wrapping. In the Middle East, where hospitality is elevated to a fine art, mothers mentor their daughters in how to be excellent hosts. In Turkmenistan, where most of the women still wear traditional dress, mothers mentor their daughters in how to sew those garments. In the US, Martha Stewart developed a whole industry around women's needs to be mentored in home management, gardening, and cooking. It's been our way as a nation to recapture many of these skills and traditions lost because of our busy lifestyle.

Mentoring is a ministry of *multiplication. The word mentoring* comes from Homer's *Odyssey.* Mentor was the trusted companion and friend of Ulysses. He became the teacher and advisor to Telemachus, the son Ulysses, while his father was fighting the Trojan War. Mentoring is not just teaching, it's also *training*. It's not just information, it's *transferring* a passion. It's not just learning, but *living* it out. Consider how Paul mentored Timothy.

- "What you've learned entrust and teach other faithful men" (2 Tim. 2:2)
- "Live like a soldier and be prepared to suffer hardship with me" (vv. 3–4)
- "Consider what I say for the Lord will give you understanding in everything" (v. 8)
- "Be diligent. Present yourself approved of God and don't be ashamed" (v15)
- "Don't be quarrelsome. Correct those in opposition with gentleness" (v 25)

While women are not strangers to mentoring, they've tended to defer to men for mentoring in business and in leadership. How many books about leadership have you read authored by women? Perhaps it's because women considered these areas traditionally a man's turf. However, with the advent of information technologies women are quickly learning how to become entrepreneurs and develop successful businesses. Today, women have more tools and opportunities for leadership than in any other time in history.

Qualities of a Good Mentor

You can learn a lot from the way Jesus mentored His disciples. He challenged them with thought-provoking questions. He spoke indirectly through parables. He probed his audience to see what was in their hearts. Sometimes His teaching was difficult to understand, which probably frustrated the disciples. Still, Jesus knew that the only way they could mature quickly in the three short years He had with them was for them to learn to think from heaven's perspective.

"But who do you that say I am?" Jesus asked His disciples during a conversation when they were pondering other people's speculations about Jesus' identity (Matt. 16:15).

To the blind man Jesus asked, "What do you want?" Why ask a blind man such an obvious question? A skillful mentor asks questions that force you to discover important truths on your *own*. Then you are able to grow, meet challenges, and find effective solutions to problems.

A friend of mine told me how a wise employer mentored her. From time to time when she was overwhelmed by a problem she would go into her employer's office to discuss it and to get his input. The employer would listen attentively while she tried to get him to take responsibility for the problem. While she talked he listened attentively. At the end of their meeting he would return the problem to the woman. The problem always went back to her. That's how she learned to take responsibility for solving her own problems.

Note also the way that Jesus responded to Judas. He never tried to rescue or warn him. Instead he said, "What you are about to do, do quickly"(John 13:27). Good mentors will not try to rescue you from your mistakes. They will give you the freedom to make an error so you can learn from it. Women, in particular, must guard against the urge to comfort others in the midst of a learning experience. Giving comfort at the wrong time can interfere with how the Lord is dealing with that person.

Look for the following qualities in a mentor:

- An active listener who hears your verbal and nonverbal communication
- One who asks questions that help you think for yourself
- One who affirms *and* challenges you to grow
- A person who has been there themselves
- One who is willing to be transparent about her own successes and failures
- One who prays for you
- A good role model

Where to Find a Mentor

While men are more accustomed to finding formal mentors, women are natural co-mentors. They don't hesitate to share their concerns and feelings openly when they are together with other women. Over the phone, with coworkers, while touching up their makeup in restrooms, over coffee with a friend—women love to bare their souls during informal peer-mentoring moments. Finding someone willing to mentor you formally might be more intimidating. Here are some possible ways to develop a formal mentoring relationship.

- Consider seniors who have lived full and productive lives and are mature Christians. Often they have fewer time restraints and enjoy encouraging younger leaders. Take time to know these people better by offering a practical service, stopping by to visit them, and praying with them. Those encounters will lead to natural opportunities to build a more formal mentoring relationship.
- Read the writings of an author whose work touches you in a special way. This approach lacks personal contact, but you can still learn a lot from the author's insights. While still a new Christian, my husband, Steve, drew much from the works of C. S. Lewis, who helped him understand the Christian life. Steve still keeps a cherished collection of Lewis's books and reads them regularly. Henri Nouwen is an author whose writings have influenced my life and thinking. Do you have an author who has struck a special chord in your heart? (Please don't say Danielle Steele!)
- Join a women's Bible study, such as Bible Study Fellowship or Precepts, led by mature Christian women. You may meet an interesting woman with whom you can develop a formal mentoring relationship. Take time to attend a women's retreat sponsored by your church. In a relaxed weekend environment, you may strike up a friendship with someone who has something to teach you. After the event, call that person and let her know you would be honored if she could mentor you in a specific area.

Elements of a Good Mentoring Plan

For many women mentoring happens informally. Take a minute to reflect on your own experiences. Look around you. Perhaps there is someone you work with who can teach you a lot simply by observing his or her actions.

Ed Dayton, former vice president-at-large of World Vision International, has been a great mentor to me over the years. He did it informally by asking probing questions such as, "And how do you plan to solve this problem?" He helped me to think strategically. He encouraged me to be a leader by believing in me and by his example as a leader with purpose and integrity.

While you can learn many things through informal relationships there are times when you need to intentionally seek a formal relationship with a mentor. Formal mentoring relationships help to refine your purpose through accountability. They give someone permission to speak into your life and help you become more focused. They help you mature faster in that specific area. Consider also that some mentors don't work with individuals, but only with small groups. It's a better investment of the mentor's time, and the group learns from one another as well.

If you would like to pursue a formal mentoring relationship with an individual or in a group, take time to define your objectives. On the next page is a sample form with suggestions of what to include in your plan.

THE ART OF MENTORING

MENTOR PLANNING FORM

Name: _____

Goals (topics to be discussed):
1. _____
2. _____
3. _____

Discussion on "Life Areas" e.g. business, sports, Christian life, etc.

How often will you meet:

Meeting location:

Meeting time and duration:

Length of mentoring relationship:

Books/texts to be used:

Method of reporting (i.e., written, verbal, etc.):

Method of accountability:

• **Reading** _____
• **Homework** _____
• **Learning activities** _____

Date of evaluation session:

Final review:

THE ART OF MENTORING

Suggested Mentoring Topics

Spiritual Development Using Bible Study and Prayer

- How to study God's Word
- Principles of intercession and spiritual warfare
- Knowing the Father heart of God
- Forgiveness—how to live it out
- Understanding God's ways
- How to live a life pleasing to God

Personal Development

- Finding your spiritual gifts
- Understanding God's call for your life
- Time management
- Biblical role of a wife
- Biblical principles for parenting
- Disciplines of the woman in Proverbs 31

Leadership Development

- Leadership styles of various Old Testament prophets
- How to develop a strategic plan
- Fundraising
- Building a prayer team
- Financial management
- How do I influence (lead) people?

Mentoring Is a Three Way Street

Learning takes place not only when we receive, but also when we give. That's why we need to cultivate receiving relationships, sharing relationships, and giving relationships. We need all three.

A Receiving Relationship

This occurs when someone more experienced than you is willing to share his or her successes and failures—in other words, what they are learning in the laboratory of life. They study your potential and are committed to helping you grow. You need this relationship because when life gets complicated—and it does for all of us—it's easy to get bogged down by the circumstances and lose your focus. It's times like these when you need someone to come alongside you and help you to develop healthy attitudes and perspectives.

A Sharing Relationship
This is by far the most common form of mentoring. This is an informal relationship between two people who are honest enough to speak the truth to each other.

Do you have someone in your life who can challenge you about bad habits without you snapping back, "Well, I don't see any wings sprouting out from your shoulders!" If you do, appreciate them; they are rare. Proverbs 27:6 describes those people this way, "Faithful are the wounds of a friend; profuse are the kisses of an enemy."

In my own experience I have found that the best way to have this type of relationship is to invite people to give me their input. As long as I respect their judgment and know they are motivated by love, not criticism, I listen when they speak. Having your blind spots pointed out isn't always comfortable. A true friend will love you enough to help you see them, and then pray with you for answers.

An Affirming Relationship
To mature, you have to learn how to give as well as receive. As you make time to mentor others, you will enrich and be enriched by the experience. "Older women likewise are to be reverent in their behavior,.that they may encourage the young women to love their husbands, to love their children, to be sensible, pure . . ." (Titus 2:3–5).

When older women take time to mentor younger ones about their roles as wives and mothers, the result is stronger marriages and healthier families. Take time to affirm others.

Summary

There is great merit in learning from others. On your own, you can be tempted to give up too soon or to overestimate the time it takes to achieve your goals. Good mentors will help you keep your reigns at exactly the right tension so you can maintain balance and keep a healthy pace in life. They will hold you accountable to your purpose. Remember to enjoy the process while you run your race. Take some advice from Gloria Gaither: "We may run, walk, stumble, drive, or fly, but let us never lose sight of the reason for the journey, or miss a chance to see a rainbow on the way."[5]

In this chapter you reviewed:

- Mentoring is a ministry of multiplication.
- Good mentors help you learn how to think for yourself.
- Mentors work with groups and individuals. Both approaches have benefits.
- Mentoring can be a receiving, sharing, or giving relationship.
- A good mentor will help refine your purpose through accountability.

Building a Strategy for Being Mentored

Katharine Graham once said,"Some questions don't have answers, which is a terribly difficult lesson to learn." This may be true, using conventional wisdom. However, instead of taking a fatalistic approach we could seize the opportunity to seek God's wisdom on the matter - to learn and grow. A good mentor can be invaluable in this regard. Here are four things I do when I need to find a mentor. I trust it will help you in build your own strategy.

1. Decide when it's time to seek the help of a mentor

My greatest need for a mentor is when I've taken on an assignment that requires knowledge outside my present scope of experience. Rather than be intimidated I've seen this as an opportunity to grow. Research in the new field becomes my first priority. Asking God for His wisdom goes without saying. That's also when I recognize the value of a mentor – someone who can steer me in the right direction. Through them I've been able to increase my learning curve and achieve my goals faster and with less trial and error. A mentor at such a moment is worth their weight in gold.

Determine your criteria for knowing it's time to seek a mentor's help.

2. Look for authors whose work speaks to your situation

Once I've identified my need for a mentor I research to find authors whose writings can educate me in my present situation. The advantage of an author is that you can access their material as often as necessary without imposing on someone's time. As a strategist I've gained invaluable insights from biographies of military generals, politicians and business strategists.

Find authors who can educate you in your area of need.

3. Connect with people in your immediate circle

I'm always amazed to discover that I don't have to look far to find help. That's the power of networking. Even if friends don't have the answer they know of someone who does and can refer me to them.

The best way to establish a relationship with a mentor is to tell them why you think they would help you and then ask if they are available to help you in a specific way. No one has ever been offended by being asked to be a mentor! If you approach someone who leads a very public life be considerate of that person's time. They may need to guard their personal time with less people-intensive commitments.

4. Seek God's wisdom for every situation

God often uses people to speak into my life but my best mentor and counsel is the Lord Himself. His Word is rich in insight and wisdom to speak to every situation.

Not long ago I received a call from Luis Bush, Director of the AD 2000 Movement and Beyond inviting me to make a plenary presentation at a major international gathering in Jerusalem, Israel. The call came during a time of intense travel for me. I was weary and was not looking forward to another international trip. But Jesus is my mentor. He has the final word on which assignments I take. When I prayed, the Lord prompted me to read Isaiah 40:2. This is what it says. *"Speak kindly to Jerusalem: And call out to her that her warfare has ended."* From that verse I sensed there was a reason for me to go to Jerusalem!

Learn to relate everything to Jesus. He has the answer to all your questions.

Read, Reflect, & Respond

These exercises will challenge you to reflect on the qualities of a good mentor and help you identify areas where you could use the help of a mentor.

Bible Study

Take a few minutes alone to read and reflect on the following Scripture. Record your thoughts in a journal.

JAMES 1:5 *But if any of you lacks wisdom, let him ask of God, who gives to all men generously and without reproach, and it will be given to him.*
Is there an area in your life that lacks wisdom? What have you been doing to address this issue? Who do you know who could help you grow in this area?

Homework Questions

Who are the people who have mentored you in the past? What made them effective or ineffective?

Small Group Question

In this chapter we reviewed three types of mentoring relationships: a receiving relationship, a peer relationship, and an affirming relationship. Which of these three areas are you presently involved in and which do you need to be involved in?

Recommended Reading
If you are studying this book as a group perhaps one or two members can read one book and bring a book summary to the group.

Connecting: The Mentoring Relationships You Need to Succeed in Life, Robert Clinton and Paul Stanley (NavPress: Colorado Springs).
Mentoring: The Strategy of the Master, Ron Lee Davis (Thomas Nelson Publishing: Nashville, Tennessee, 1991).
Women Connecting with Women, Verna Birkey (WinePress Publishing: Enumclaw, Washington).

Read, Reflect & Respond

Chapter Three

♦ ♦ ♦

Know Your Limits

Focus Your Purpose by Setting Boundaries and Priorities

The whole point of getting things done is knowing what to leave undone.

—Lady Stella Reading

Know Your Limits
Focus Your Purpose by Setting Boundaries and Priorities

"Dear Lord, You created me with wonder and delight in my soul. Why then should I go through life anxious and serious seeking to get ahead, striving to make ends meet? I rush and hurry, filling up my calendar. Where is the joy? Where are the days of summer rest? Where is my sense of delight? Joyful Lord, help me unclutter my life and make room for Your joy. Help me find purpose and know Your priorities so, in the end, my life will bring joy to Your heart."

Commentary

A professor at a business college came to class one day with a big one-gallon jar. He began to put rocks into it until there was no room left. Then he asked, "How many of you think this jar is full and can't hold anything else?"

All the students raised their hands.

Then the professor reached down and pulled out a sack of gravel and poured it into the jar. The gravel filtered down and filled the space between the rocks. Then the professor asked, "How many of you think this jar is full now?

Nobody answered.

The professor then reached down and took a bag of sand and poured it into the jar. It sifted through the rocks and the gravel. Again he asked if the jar was full.

Again, no one answered.

Finally, he took a jar of water and poured it over the contents of the jar, filling every remaining space until the jar overflowed.

Then the professor asked one final question, "What is the moral of this story?"

One student raised his hand and asked, "Is it that there is always more room in our schedule than we think there is?"

"No," replied the professor. "The moral of this story is to put the big rocks in *first*."

That story is about priorities. In this chapter you will learn why priorities are important and how to make them a part of your daily life.

Priorities are Essential to Leadership

Success can be defined as the progressive realization of a predetermined goal. This definition tells us that the discipline to prioritize and the ability to work toward a stated goal are essential to a leader's success.[6]

Before you can achieve anything in life – big or small – you need to have an idea of:

- What you need to accomplish
- How and when you want to get there
- Your work style

Everyone needs to have goals for their work, their home, and their personal life. Without goals your decisions and actions are governed and driven by external forces, instead of your own goals and priorities. Without clear goals you sail "reactively" through life on a road that takes you nowhere. You spend a huge amount of time on things of little importance and too much time spinning your wheels in an endless circle.

When goals and priorities drive your actions, you live "proactively." Your goals become a "roadmap" steering you where you want to go and how you want to get there. Learning to set and live by clear goals and priorities is an indispensable discipline of leadership. If this discipline is so important, why do so many people fail to use it in their daily lives?

Roadblocks to Planning

Because women carry out multiple roles—wife, mother, "domestic goddess", career woman, caregiver — they can easily be consumed by the demands of those roles and forget to set specific goals for their own lives.

During times of crisis most people *instinctively* know their priorities and execute them with remarkable resourcefulness. A sense of urgency causes them to become very productive. However, when the crisis is over and the routine of life returns, they are tempted to fall back to old ways.

There is an art and science to living a focused life. When you haven't understood the benefits of planning you are tempted to live your life with excuses that justify your behavior. Here are three common ones:

Procrastination

"All hard work brings a profit, but mere talk leads only to poverty" (Prov. 14:23). If you struggle with procrastination, the cause may be rooted in one of the following:

- Guilt for overlooking a task
- Fear of failure or success
- Being intimidated or overwhelmed by the task
- A lifestyle of complacency, a lack of motivation
- A habit of rationalizing
- Unclear about priorities, overlooking what's important

Disorganization

"He will die for lack of discipline, led astray by his own great folly" (Prov. 5:23). If you are constantly disorganized, consider some of these reasons:

- Unmotivated about your life
- Overwhelmed by too much clutter
- Mentally or emotionally stressed or confused
- Lacking in personal goals

Over-commitment

"If I were still trying to please men, I would not be a servant of Christ" (Gal. 1:10). People who overextend do so because they:

- Have difficulty saying no
- Allow others to control them
- Give up rest and leisure
- Feel guilty when not working
- Enjoy making long lists

Do any of these conditions describe you? The principles and exercises in this chapter will give you the tools to move beyond these obstacles and into a new freedom.

Establishing Goals

If you are like most people, you have a long list of goals - all of them important yet far too many to reasonably achieve them at once. Most women's "to do" lists look like this: Cook meals, run the kids to school, go to work, buy groceries, do the laundry, teach Bible study, care for aging parents. Even the model woman in Proverbs 31 had her hands full. Consider some of her responsibilities.

- EARLY RISER: "She rises also while it is still night, and gives food to her household" (v. 15).
- INVESTOR: "She considers a field and buys it. From her earnings she plants a vineyard" (v. 16).
- DONOR: "She extends her hand to the poor and stretches out her hand to the needy" (v. 20).
- SEAMSTRESS: "She makes coverings for herself" (v. 22).
- ENTREPRENEUR: She makes linen garments and sells them (v. 24).

How do you lead a busy life and still maintain a sense of order in your life? The answer is simple. Set clear goals and live by them. Consider these questions as you set your goals:

- What do I want from my **work and my place of ministry?**
- What do I want to accomplish at **home**?
- What do I want to do for **myself?**

Once you've made your list ask yourself the following questions about the goals you've established:

- Does the Lord want me to have this goal?
- Am I willing to do what it takes to achieve it?
- Do I have the necessary skills and experience to achieve this goal?

Let's say one of your goals is to start a small home-based business to supplement income for the family. When you ask yourself the question, "Does the Lord want me to have this goal?" the answer needs to be yes. If you aren't sure, step back and find out before you move ahead.

Your next question is to decide if you are prepared to devote enough *time* to see the business grow – building your customer base, marketing your product, understanding the competition, keeping accounting records and so on.

Finally, you need to decide if you have enough training to do the job. If not, you may want to take some training *before* you launch your business.

When you set goals, keep in mind the following guidelines. Goals must be –

- Specific and measurable. Vague statements like "I want to make money" are not measurable.
- Realistic. If you are 80 years old it may be too late to become an opera singer!
- Flexible. Goals are not carved in stone. Just as life changes so will your goals.
- Put it in writing. It helps you remember it and allows you to review it frequently.
- Manageable. If the goal is big, like "clean the house" break it into smaller sub-goals that are manageable such as listing what you will do in each room in the house.
- Cross off your goals when you accomplish them. It will encourage you to consider your next goal.[7]

Your planning strategy looks like this:

- How you live your life is determined by your *goals.*
- What goals we choose are determined by your *priorities.*
- Whether we reach our goals is determined by your *planning.*

Your next step is priorities.

Determine Your Priorities

Priorities define those things in your life that are important to you. They are driven by your values. They include what you want to accomplish at work, in your home and in your personal life. Decide what is important to you and in what order. Write them down.

Knowing your priorities and following them are two different things. If you lead a busy life you face many demands on your time. As those demands grow it's easy for some of your priorities to be overlooked and take a back burner position. Several years ago I realized that I had allowed my professional priorities to consume all of my time to the neglect of many of my personal priorities. My life became out of balance. I became very ill and was bedridden for several weeks. During that time I was able to re-evaluate my life and begin to put my personal priorities in their proper perspective. We need to develop priorities for *every* area of our lives.

Once you've made your list use the ABC method to determine the order by which you will carry out each priority.

Those items that need doing first are the **A priorities.**
Mark items than can wait as **C priorities.**
All the remaining items left on your list are your **B priorities.**

Here are some questions to ask:

- Does this request fit in my priorities?
- Am I the right person to assume responsibility for this task or assignment?
- Can someone else do this task? If so who?

Just because you are capable of doing something doesn't mean you are the one to do it!

Build an Action Plan

Now that you know your goals and the order of priority you will pursue them, it's time to build an *action plan* to help you carry this out. Your action plan shows how you intend to achieve your goals and establishes a deadline for doing them. Here you will need a calendar to remind you of your commitments. It needs to be portable enough to carry with you to record and remind you of your commitments wherever you go. If you enjoy modern technology, the handheld PDAs (personal digital assistant) are more than a calendar. They offer an address book, phone book, memo pad, birthday reminders, and other organizational tools.

As you plan your priorities consider the 80/20 rule: 80 percent of your results come from 20 percent of your efforts. Set aside time each month to determine your monthly priorities, then schedule them in your calendar. First tackle those priorities that yield 80% of your results. The aim here is not to work hard but smart.

Let's look at the example of the home-based business. You can spend hours organizing your office and acquiring new products. These are important priorities but your 80% rule is to build your customer base. Customers are the engine of your business. The other areas help maintain that engine. When you schedule your priorities you will also need to indicate how *many* customers you'll need by which *date*. That way you can see your business grow in monthly increments.

My Personal Planning System

Over the years I have developed a very simple planning system. At the beginning of each year I take time to prayerfully consider my goals and their priority for that year. These include goals for my work and ministry, my home and my areas of personal and spiritual development. Then I post these in my office and keep a copy in my planning journal.

At the beginning of each month I review these goals and decide *how* I will execute them during that month. My monthly goals include goals for all three areas – work, home, and personal. They set the tone for that month. Some months I spend the majority of my time traveling and speaking. Other months I am in the office writing and conducting meetings. Still others I spend networking, meeting people and building new relationships. There is a rhythm to each month.

The monthly goals dictate my weekly priorities. I try to tackle my most challenging priorities first, especially in the morning hours when I have my most creative energy. I allow 15 minute breaks throughout the day to mull over what I am doing, to quietly pray for continued wisdom for my work, or to return phone calls. Then I'm back on track working my plan. Any items that don't get accomplished for that day become a priority for the following day.

If I am not traveling or speaking on Sundays I will use this day to spend time with the Lord and in worship at church. I'll take a brief nap in the afternoon and use the rest of the day to be with my family and do something creative or rejuvenating.

This is what works for me. Whatever system you use it should serve your needs. The simpler the system, the more likely you are to use it.

Build Systems That Unclutter Your Life

As you become efficient in setting goals and priorities, you will discover time wasters that clutter your life. To eliminate these nonessentials and win the war, you will need time on your side. Develop systems that help you organize and eliminate clutter, and incorporate them in your daily schedule. For example, if you subscribe to newspapers or newsletters read them as soon as they arrive, or at least go through them for articles you may need to read later. Cut out the articles, date them, and place them in a reading file. Give yourself no more than one week to read the article. At the end of the week if you haven't read it, throw it out.

Do you remember the last time you cleaned out your closets? Did you feel a weight lift from your shoulders as order once again resumed in your house? Now consider the four areas where clutter accumulates in your life:

- The number of belongings you possess
- Your use of space at home and at work—including your furniture layout
- The flow of paper and electronic information
- The way you spend your time

To bring order to those areas, you need *a plan* that will help you sort out each area systematically. Remember, just chose one area and make it work. Then try another. There is great reward is setting small goals and achieving them.

The less you own, the easier it is to maintain and organize everything. Women sometimes hold onto things for sentimental reasons. If you don't need that memorabilia but hate to part with it, why not take a photo of it and then give it away? The photo will remind you of its sentimental value, but your life will be free of clutter.

Have you noticed that the areas with the most clutter in your home are full of the things you enjoy the least? Filing, doing the dishes, gardening, housework—which is yours? One strategy is to do those chores using a time limit that forces you to move through the assignment fairly quickly. Here are a few more suggestions for bringing order and keeping your home uncluttered. Again, chose *one* area and make it work before trying to tackle the next. Delegate some of the assignments to members of your family so everyone participates in keeping the home organized.

- Designate a place for everything. Store things there.
- Establish a recycling program for your mail, food, and clothing. Sort incoming mail as soon as it arrives. Keep what you want and toss the rest in the recycle bin. Place bills in one file, letters in another, reading material separately. Plan to review each within twenty-four hours.
- Sort through your wardrobe twice a year and remove clothes you no longer need.
- Ruthlessly recycle. Bless others by letting them enjoy what you don't need.
- Establish a cleaning routine. Delegate tasks to family members or to a cleaning service.
- Systematically rearrange furniture, equipment, and other components in your home and office to create more room and order.

Office Organization

The same approach applies to your office. Organize your furniture in a way that allows for maximum space and traffic flow. Make sure you have good lighting. Review your records annually and only keep those items that you currently need. Toss or archive the rest. Don't hold onto paperwork longer than you need. Approach every piece of mail that comes to your office in one of four ways.
1. Read and toss
2. File
3. Place in a follow-up file for further action
4. Delegate to someone else.

Keep in mind these tips, strategies and timesaving techniques:
1. Make all your phone calls at one time.
2. Minimize interruptions. Discourage visitors politely if your culture permits.
3. Hire the best people.

4. Unclutter your desk. Keep only those items you are working on.
5. Create workable files.
6. Set written goals and priorities.
7. Use lists. Write down what you need to do and check it off as you do it.
8. Do the worst first.
9. Learn to delegate.
10. Take care of the small stuff at once.[8]

To help you further develop effective organizational systems that meet your needs, review the reading resources listed at the end of this chapter.

Summary

Make a regular habit of setting priorities in your life. It will help you become purposeful and focused. There is great satisfaction in setting goals and reaching them. If God simply handed things to you, it would rob you of the joy of accomplishment. But it takes time to develop this discipline. Remember these principles:

- Allow God to dictate the priorities of your life.
- Identify and seek to overcome habits that hinder you from honoring your goals.
- Make time to plan your goals.
- Learn to say no.
- Spend 20 percent of your time on those goals that yield 80 percent of your results.
- Build simple systems that keep your life uncluttered.

Building a Strategy
For Organization

Do you feel you have found a system of planning and organization that works for you? If you haven't, this chapter provides a number of simple tools to help you develop your goals and build effective action plans. Take time to review your existing goals and plans and to write new ones using the following simple system.

1. What are my goals for this year – for work and ministry, home and personal development?
2. In what order of priority will I carry out these goals?
3. How effectively am I working my action plan on a weekly basis?
4. What changes do I need to make to my home in order to have better organization and management? How will I do it? When will I do it?

5. Is my office layout serving my needs? Do I need to change anything?
6. How efficient are my office systems? How can I improve my office efficiency?

If you can answer these questions you are well on your way to living within your boundaries and priorities.

Read, Reflect, & Respond

The following questions are designed to help you better identify your organizational needs.

Bible Study

Take a few minutes to read and reflect on the following Scripture.

- PROVERBS 1:7. *The fear of the Lord is the beginning of knowledge; fools despise wisdom and instruction.*
  The fear of the Lord can be translated to mean *the reverence of God and His ways.* Using this interpretation, how does your reverence for God give you wisdom for choosing your goals?

Homework Questions

Is there an area in your life that weighs you down, consumes more time than you want? What can you do to delegate or diminish its demand?

Small Group Questions

Talk about tips, strategies, and time saving techniques that help you manage your time and your life. Try to learn one new tip from someone else.

Recommended Reading

The Way of the Heart, Henri Nouwen (Ballantine Books: New York, 1981).
Tyranny of the Urgent, Charles E. Hummel (InterVarsity Press, Downers Grove, IL.1994 – Paperback)
How to Get Things Done (National Press Publication, a division of Rockhurst College Continuing Education Center, Inc., 1998.
How to De-Junk Your Life (National Press Publication, a division of Rochhurst College Continuing Education Center, Inc., 1998.

Chapter Four

Integrity

Identify Your Purpose through Honesty

Y ou teach a little by
what you say. You teach a
lot by what you are.

—*Dr. Henrietta Mears*

Integrity
Identify Your Purpose through Honesty

Lord, make me childlike. Deliver me from the urge to compete with others for place or prestige or position. I would be simple as a little child. Deliver me from pose and pretense. Forgive me for thinking of myself. Help me to forget myself and find my true peace in beholding You. That You may answer this prayer, I humble myself before You. Lay upon me Your easy yoke of self-forgetfulness, that through it I may find rest. Amen.

—A. W. Tozer

Commentary

In the mid 1980s, Leona Helmsley developed a reputation for owning and managing some of the finest five-star hotels in the US. Her outstanding commitment to service and her impeccable attention to detail were legendary. This she accomplished at considerable cost to, and abuse of her staff, who nicknamed her "Queen of Mean." Whenever the queen set foot on the premises, terror reigned. Just a speck of detectable dust was sufficient ground for dismissal.

But not only did she deny her employees fair treatment; she also tried to defraud the government of taxes. She coined the statement "Only the little people pay taxes." It was just a matter of time until her arrogance and dishonesty caught up with her. She was arrested, fined, and publicly humiliated. Today, Leona Helmsley may be a free woman, but her reputation and the public's respect for her have been lost forever. She exemplifies a person who lacks integrity.

INTEGRITY

Integrity Defined

- (In-teg-ri-ty) *n.* Soundness, honesty, completeness.
- LATIN: integer; "whole."
- HEBREW: taman; "to be upright, whole, complete."

What is integrity? In short, it is *truth* and the ability to be truthful. When you live in truth you become a free person. That freedom allows you to be transparent; you have nothing to hide. Truth demands that you refuse to put on a front for others. Truthful people are honest and *humble* enough to be the same in public as they are in private.

Jesus promised, "You shall know the truth and the truth will set you free" (John 8:32). His truth frees you to become the person He created you to be. It also frees you from the fear of death. You know your final destiny. Martyrs who chose to die for their faith demonstrated they were free in life and in death.

The opposite of integrity is dishonesty or deception. Dishonesty imprisons you because you need to hide. You have to be guarded. You can't be spontaneous. Losing your integrity is like losing your soul. Without it you can't grow in your relationship with the Lord. You also lose your *influence* as a leader.

Integrity is a practical issue. It's not just what you say, it's who you are. As Henrietta Mears, founder of Gospel Light International would say, "You teach a little by what you say. You teach the most by what you are." Before you can begin to be honest with others, you must learn to be honest with yourself.

Behaviors of Low Integrity

One way to be cured of a vice is to see how unsightly it looks when reflected in the lives of others. British television cleverly captures that aspect in a humorous series called *Keeping Up Appearances.*

The show revolves around Richard and Hyacinth Bucket, a middle-class English couple who become the laughingstock of friends and neighbors when Hyacinth insists on passing herself off as having upper-class breeding. Her acquaintances secretly call her "the *bucket* woman," but Hyacinth always pronounces her last name as *"Bouquet!"*

Hyacinth frequently makes statements like, "People who try to pretend they are superior make it so much harder for those of us who really are!" Or she'll exasperate her husband and say, "Richard, there is absolutely no reason to ask for something very expensive if nobody is listening." Never mind that the item is totally out of their price range. She's also known to say, "Someone has to fly the flag of finesse around here." That's an amusing comment when it comes from someone who is totally insensitive to others. The show makes for hilarious comedy. But it also reveals how foolish pretentiousness can look.

INTEGRITY

Dishonesty and pretense are weighty matters. They creep undetected into your life. To have credibility as a leader you must be prepared to face your dishonesty so that it doesn't permeate your values and life. Take a minute to review the following behaviors. See if any are reflected in your life.

DECEPTIVE BEHAVIOR
Dressing and acting seductively
    for the opposite sex
Gossiping

Living beyond your means
Exaggeration and lying
Secretiveness from your spouse
Undermining authority

WRONG MOTIVE
Gaining illicit attention

casual/malicious/envious/jealous/
    competitive spirit
The need to impress others
The need for approval
Selfish desires
Refusing to submit

One Woman's Price for Losing Her Integrity
Strikingly beautiful, vital, and charismatic was how most people described Mary. She came from a fine Christian family and was a professing Christian. Her many talents led her to win a beauty contest. Soon she began to move among the circles of the rich and famous. In spite of her rising career as an actress, inwardly she began to seek affirmation through marriage.

Mary thought she could use her beauty to secure her desire. A handsome actor began dating her. When he refused to meet her timetable for marriage, the rejection led her to turn to another man. He promised marriage, and that led to one sexual encounter with him. However, he deceived her. Mary was left with only the AIDS virus. It was a wake-up call that struck her like a bad dream—except it was real life.

Mary realized her desperate search for a husband caused her to lose her life's purpose. She humbled herself before the Lord and asked her parents for their forgiveness. Today, she has a vital ministry to young women in high schools, beauty pageants, and churches—wherever she can find them. She warns about the dangers of flirting with sex. She endures constant pain because of her condition, but she is totally committed to living with integrity in spite of the price she paid to get it.

The moral of this true story? Don't compromise your integrity or seek a shortcut to your goal. In addition to many consequences, it could derail your life's purpose.

Building Integrity Day by Day

In his book *The 21 Irrefutable Laws of Leadership,* John Maxwell defines the Law of Process as an important law for building leadership. He says, "Leadership is developed daily, not in a day."[9] The same principle applies to integrity. It's a daily discipline of learning to live in honesty and owning your attitude and actions. Some things come easily. Others are a struggle. Build a plan to help you stay honest. The following are some principles that will help.

1. Renew Your Mind
Learn to be a steward of your thoughts.

- "As a man thinks in his heart so is he." (Prov. 23:7)
- "And be not conformed to this world, but be transformed by the renewing of your mind." (Rom. 12:2)

Take time each day to examine your heart. Ask the Lord to show you the areas where you lack integrity. When He does, repent and renew your mind with Scriptures that confirm you are strong in that area..

Then ask God to give you a healthy fear of Him. "The fear of the Lord is the beginning of wisdom" (Prov. 9:10). In your desire to please God your heart will be opened to the Holy Spirit's prompting and you will learn wisdom to conduct yourself in godly integrity. For example, you may be talking about someone when the Holy Spirit says, "Uh-uh. Don't say that!" That's the time to stop, take a deep breath, and change the subject.

At the end of each day ask the Lord to show you how obedient you were to His directions. Make it a daily habit, and you'll be sure to walk in integrity.

2. Seek a Mentor
Old habits die hard. That's why it helps to ask someone you trust to come alongside and help hold you accountable. That person can give you honest feedback, and encourage you in your journey. Sometimes knowing that you have to share frankly your choices with someone else motivates you to try harder. (Refer to Chapter 2, *The Art of Mentoring,* for guidelines.)

3. Build Your Integrity Muscles
Integrity takes time to develop. Make it a lifelong discipline that helps you stay the course with honesty and consistency. Integrity comes when you keep doing what you know you are supposed to do, whether anyone is watching or not. That kind of discipline brings inner affirmation. When you are consistent in living in truth, it will have an impact in producing godly character that the Lord will approve of and others will recognize and trust.

Integrity: The Essence of Leadership

In today's world of contradicting values, people often confuse public favor with character. Society's approval is meaningless if the leader's personal life lacks integrity. God is our final judge, and that's where the true nature of our character will be revealed.

During the early 1970s I had the privilege of singing in the choir of a remarkable woman named Kathryn Kuhlman. Kathryn's motto was "I believe in miracles!" She lived her life in the miraculous. Her monthly miracle services at the Shrine Auditorium in Los Angeles packed in five thousand people, with an overflow of two thousand hopefuls waiting to be seated. From every walk of life they came seeking a miracle from God.

When Kathryn Kuhlman stepped on the platform, God's presence was tangible. You could almost touch it. The results were visible. I saw large goiters on people shrink before my eyes. Thousands of blind and deaf people received their sight and hearing. I saw hundreds of crippled people get up from their wheelchairs and slowly regain their mobility. I saw deformed people transformed before my eyes. By the end of each meeting, there wasn't a "Doubting Thomas" in the auditorium. Atheists became believers, and agnostics discovered that Jesus was real. In her meetings, lives were radically transformed and many came to faith.

Less than a year after I joined Miss Kuhlman's choir, the Lord called her home to be with Him. During those brief ten months, I learned that there is no end to what God will do if we dare to believe Him for miracles. However, the most profound impact on my life came in a brief statement Kathryn Kuhlman made a few weeks before her death. She was asked how she prepared for those remarkable healing services. Her answer was simple but profound: "I don't prepare at all. I stay prepared!" Her example of integrity inspired other Christian leaders to seek consistency in their own ministry.

Summary

"Hype and appearance. That is the type of generation we live in," writes author and pastor Earl Palmer in his book *Integrity in a World of Pretense*. "Integrity has taken a beating in this modern world of ours, as we know from watching the nightly news. Even the religious has had its share of scandals. Somehow, our Christian senses have been deadened by all the glitz and noise. And somehow it has made our quest to live a life consistent with the gospel more and more difficult."[10]

Here is what we have reviewed in this chapter:

- Integrity is truth and the ability to live in it.
- To be honest with others you must first be honest with yourself.

- Integrity gives you credibility as a leader.
- A lack of integrity will lead you to a pattern of deceptive behaviors.
- You build integrity by:
    - Renewing your mind through God's Word
    - Inviting honest feedback from a mentor
    - Making integrity a lifelong discipline

Building Your Strategy for Integrity

Peter Drucker, the management expert, makes this distinction between being clever and being credible. "The final requirement of effective leadership is to earn trust. Otherwise there won't be any followers…A leader is someone who has followers. To trust a leader, it is *not* necessary to agree with him. It is a belief in something very old-fashioned called 'integrity' A leader's actions and a leader's professed beliefs must be congruent or at least compatible. Effective leadership - and again this is very old wisdom – is not based on being clever; it is based primarily on being consistent."[11]

The integrity of an organization is governed by how well it lives up to its stated core values. This is a system of values against which it has elected to be measured. You too can also develop a set of core values against which all your actions are measured. It can become a checkpoint for helping you build consistency in your life. It can be a mirror that reflects your level of integrity, humility and honesty.

Take a few minutes and write out your list of core values. These are beliefs, values and convictions for which you are not prepared to compromise. (If you completed the questionnaire on page 10 review what you've written for your core values.)

Ask someone who knows you well to comment where they see consistencies and inconsistencies in your life. Take responsibility for areas you lack consistency and ask them to hold you accountable in those areas. As you walk the path of integrity let the words of Hebrews 12:1-2 cheer you along.

"Therefore, since we have so great a cloud of witnesses surrounding us, let us lay aside every encumbrance, and the sin which so easily entangles us, and let us run with endurance the race that is set before us, fixing our eyes on Jesus, the author and perfecter of our faith…"

It's the race of your life with a great reward waiting for you at the finishing line!

Read, Reflect, & Respond

The goal of these exercises is to help you identify where you lack integrity so you can build consistency in those areas. Only the Lord knows your heart as it really is and He can help you see it. If you cannot find inconsistencies in your life ponder these questions for a few days. God rewards those who diligently seek Him.

Bible Study

Take a few minutes alone to read and reflect on the following Scripture. Record your thoughts in a journal.

1. PROVERBS 16:2. *All the ways of a man are clean in his own sight, but the Lord weighs the motives*.
Make a list of principles you value in your life. Review this list and mark those areas where you fail to follow them. Ask the Holy Spirit to help you here.

Homework Questions

How do you plan to build consistency in the areas of your life where you lack integrity?

Small Group Questions

Have you ever been in a situation where you were asked to do something that went against principles or you felt it was dishonest. How did you respond?

Recommended Reading

Dream Big: The Henrietta Mears Story, Earl O. Roe, ed. (Regal Books, a division of Gospel Light: Ventura, California, 1990) A woman's story of vision and integrity.

Integrity in a World of Pretense, Earl Palmer (InterVarsity Press: Downer's Grove, Illinois, 1992). Insights on integrity from the Book of Philippians.

Chapter Five

◆ ◆ ◆

A Call to Excellence

Pursue Your Purpose with Self-Discipline

If you faint in the day of adversity, your strength is small.

—Proverbs 24:10

A Call to Excellence
Pursue Your Purpose with Self-Discipline

Lord, in my own strength I can do nothing. It's Your faithfulness that teaches me how to be faithful. It's Your acceptance that gives me the courage to grow. It's Your joy that gives me strength when I'm weak. Blessed Lord, I place my hand in Yours as I learn to walk in the ways of a true disciple. Amen.

Commentary

She was an excellent photographer. Very quick, perceptive, with an eye for capturing angles, glances, and nuances of color. Watching her work was seeing an artist in action. Her personal life was another story: broken relationships, unpaid bills, frequent car accidents. She was highly disciplined in one area, out of control in another—a life of contradiction.

My friend is not alone in her predicament. Each of us struggles in some area of self-control and self-discipline. I guess it's part of having an Achilles heel, of being human. Some disciplines we learn to master early in life, while others are a lifelong challenge. What causes that? Perhaps if we try to examine some of our motivations, we can understand why we struggle with certain disciplines.

A CALL TO EXCELLENCE

Three Fears That Cause Procrastination

Few of us are born with the motivation for self-discipline. In time you realize that an undisciplined life results in lost opportunity—failed exams, missed deadlines, unprepared presentations. Others succeed while you watch from the sidelines wondering why you aren't a part of the action. What often separates you from those who succeed is *not* talent or genius. It may be a lack of persistence and preparation.

Self-discipline isn't how much you do, but a commitment to doing the right things. That may be easier said than done, especially if doing the right things takes extra effort. So you procrastinate.

- "I'll start my diet tomorrow." Yet, tomorrow brings new excuses why you should delay changing your eating habits.
- "I don't feel like sorting the mail. I'll review it later." Ten days later the pile has grown to overwhelming proportions. "Where did all this mail come from?"
- "I'll study after I watch this TV program." Who feels like studying after sitting on the couch for four hours?

Procrastination means you know what you need to do and you don't do it. If you don't know what to do, you aren't procrastinating. Your are simply *thinking*. True procrastination paralyzes. It feeds on fears that are mostly unfounded. You start by believing a lie and the longer you wait to challenge that lie, the more difficult it is to get started. If you struggle with procrastination, perhaps you have allowed one of the following fears to dominate you.

1. Fear of Failure

Behind the fear of failure is the lie that you aren't good enough to succeed or that the challenge is too big. Neither is true. Most big successes rarely happen the first time. Multiple attempts are your stepping stones to success. When you accept that truth you will not be intimidated by the fear of failure. You will see your mistakes as friends, not as foes, giving you valuable insights for the future.

Fear paralyzed Judy the first time she spoke publicly. Making presentations was a requirement in her job description. She had no choice. How could five short steps to the podium cause such anxiety? To overcome her intimidation Judy began telling jokes. Not a good idea! By the time her presentation was over she had gotten off track and lost her focus. The audience never got the message, and Judy often ended up humiliated.

Rather than focus on her embarrassment Judy began analyzing her mistakes. "I think I know why I failed in my presentation," she told her team. "I relied too much on memory and not enough on preparation." At her next presentation Judy over-prepared and spent most of the time *reading* her notes out loud instead of looking at the audience. At least, this time she kept her focus but her delivery was rather dry.

Each time Judy made a presentation she asked for feedback from her team and took notes. The feedback was honest and sometimes painful. In time, Judy's patience paid off. With practice and preparation, she became a great communicator and won the respect of her team.

This story reflects three principles that will help you overcome the fear of failure:

- Face your fears and you will overcome them
- Build on the lessons learned from your mistakes
- Don't equate failure with rejection

2. Fear of Success

Several years ago, a friend of mine turned down a lucrative job in a big city. Her reason was that if she became successful, her life would change and her small town friends would no longer relate to her. Now she wonders if she missed the chance of a lifetime and feels she is too old to pursue her dreams.

Why do people fear success? Perhaps it's because they believe success will change their lives. Some people don't like change, even when it's for the better. Success brings new demands and new choices. You may lose control over some things. But you will grow as a person. To grow, you have to be willing to embrace change. Change will also stretch your faith and will give you new areas to trust in God! God promises that if you live by His word you will be successful.

This book of the law shall not depart from your mouth. But you shall meditate on it day and night, so that you may be careful to do according to all that is written in it. For then you will make your way prosperous, and then you will have success. (Joshua 1:8)

3. Fear of Taking Risks

Katherine Graham felt like the least likely candidate to become the president of the *Washington Post*. Her husband, who ran the company, had just died. She explained: "It was in the 1960s. That's when women were expected to 'please a man, catch a man, and keep a man.' They were not raised or trained for executive leadership."

With much fear and trepidation Katherine accepted her deceased husband's position. In time, she discovered that her training as a journalist had given her important insights that proved invaluable to her new role. Today, she is respected as one of America's foremost women leaders.

On the other hand, some people are risk takers by nature. They love the adrenaline that comes with facing a new challenge. They take comfort in the adage

"Nothing ventured, nothing gained." It doesn't mean that they don't feel apprehension; they have their moments of fear. But they don't allow their emotions to dictate their actions. They do what needs to be done whether they feel like it or not. They see a risk not as something to be avoided, but as a window into the future.

Even if you aren't challenge - oriented by nature, you can learn to step out and take initiative in areas where God is leading. The process of developing self-discipline requires that you venture into the new vistas that cause you to grow. When you follow God's leading, rest assured that the risks He asks you to take are divinely appointed. Whether you know it or not, He has *prepared* you for that moment. Whether people accept you or not, you are fulfilling *His* purpose. Your responsibility is to be *obedient* and to trust the Lord for the outcome.

Finding Motivation
For Self Discipline

When you study the lives of great men and women, you discover that the first victory they won was over themselves. They made self-discipline a way of life.

A person can always go through life blaming their personal failures on one thing or another. Anyone can find an excuse, but it takes a positive attitude to find a way to go over, around, under and through an obstacle that stands in your way.[12]

There is no way around it. Self-discipline is hard work. To achieve what you want out of life you have to be willing to do things you don't really want to do. To be a leader you must develop disciplines that help you stay focused and purposeful. For example, you have to exercise if you want to stay strong and healthy. You must learn to say no if you want to honor your priorities. To win the race you must first show up for practice. Motivation for self-discipline comes by keeping your goal in front of you. There is no such thing as a "free lunch."

Quick fixes don't always solve problems in the long run either. That's why crash diets don't work. Self-discipline is a *process* and the *process* is just as important as the end result. It teaches you valuable lessons that ultimately change your life and give you a new attitude when the fruit of self-discipline finally arrives.

A Stellar Example

I am fascinated by the life of the prophet Daniel. Scripture describes him as a man who had an *excellent spirit*. Although he was only human, Daniel's devotion to God made him fearless and able to stop the mouths of lions. King Darius sought Daniel's counsel and sent a decree that affected all the peoples and nations under his rule. Behind Daniel's achievements was a disciplined life totally dedicated to

God. Daniel regularly abstained from eating rich foods so he could focus on prayer. Those disciplines gave him clarity of mind, spiritual discernment, and physical strength – not to mention a handsome physique! For Daniel, self-discipline was a way of life.

If you take small steps in self-discipline now, then the day will come when it will be so much a part of you that you won't even consider it a discipline. The writer of Hebrews reminds us that "All discipline for the moment seems not to be joyful, but sorrowful. Afterward it yields the peaceful fruit of righteousness" (Heb. 12:11).

When I need encouragement for self-discipline I motivate myself through principles rather than through emotions. No one "feels like" getting up at 3 o'clock in the morning to catch an international flight! When I was single I had to say "no" to proposals of marriage many times in order to follow the Lord's call on my life. It made my mother furious to see me turn down excellent prospects but it was the right thing to do at the time. I stopped dating to keep my life simple!

Over the years I've memorized a number of affirmations. They help me gain motivation whenever I need it. Here are a few of them:

"I can do all things through Christ who strengthens me."
"Failure is not an option here!"
"A ship in the harbor is safe. But that's not what ships were made for."
"A champion never gives up!"
"Find joy in everything you do"

I have an aunt who is an opera singer. She was awarded the First Lady of Opera in New York in 1977. When I lived in Europe I had the privilege to hear her sing. During most of her performances she would bring a shouting audience to their feet. Her voice was so powerful it shattered chandeliers. What amazed me about my aunt was the disciplined life she led when she was *not* performing. She had to sleep 10 hours a day. She observed a special diet. In cold weather she avoided the outdoors. Before stepping on the stage she would kneel and pray. Every minute of her life was dedicated to preserving her voice so she could excel as a performer. She chose to live under enormous restrictions so she could attain the pinnacle of success that few enjoy. She chose to live by principle not by emotion.

Successful people are willing to do things unsuccessful people will not do [B]

Whenever I attempt a new discipline, and that's quite often, I use the following strategy:

- I acknowledge to the Lord that I can't do it alone and invite His help.
- When I fall off the "wagon" I use my affirmations to get right back up again.

- If I keep failing I seek help from others to find the pathway of least resistance.
- I evaluate my progress and give myself small breaks to mull things over.
- I reward myself for victories.

The Reward Of Self-discipline

Verle is a Christian woman who comes from a small church in Maryland. She is rather quiet, genuine, and never seeks to draw attention to herself. But when she stands to sing she is transformed into a different person. Her deep love for Jesus and her years of singing come together into a powerful union. Verle can take a known hymn and sing it with such love and passion that it brings tears to your eyes. In minutes she brings you into the Lord's presence, where you are content to stay for hours. Verle's singing looks effortless, but what you witness is the fruit of a life of devotion and self-discipline.

Most people envy Bill Gates's success, but few know the disciplined life he leads. While other billionaires might bask in the limelight of their success, Bill keeps working long hours to achieve his goal to put a personal computer—and his software—in every home. Today, Gates is one of the world's richest men. He still works long hours, even though he doesn't need more money. He enjoys exploring the possibilities of innovation.

The reward of self-discipline is excellence. It is making a difficult task look easy, giving it dignity. It is being the best you can be in a particular field no matter how high or low, no matter how small or obscure. That's what brings purpose to your life.

Summary

Many years ago, Theodore Roosevelt warned the American people about the perils of living undisciplined lives. "The things that will destroy America are prosperity at any price, peace at any price, safety first instead of duty first, the love of soft living, and the get-rich-quick theory of life."[14] The president's words still challenge us today. The world belongs to the disciplined, to those willing to pay the price to reach their goals.

Vision is one of the best motivators for self-discipline. That's why Scripture says, "without a vision the people go without restraint" (prov. 29:18). Seek God for a vision and your motivation for discipline will increase.

On the other hand, if you tend to overwork, your challenge is to develop the discipline of saying no. Thomas Merton once said, "The imagination should be allowed a certain amount of time to browse around." Rest is just as important a priority as work. It is during times of relaxation that we find ourselves open to reflection that can inspire us to creative thinking.

In this chapter you reviewed:

- Self-discipline isn't how much you do, but a commitment to doing the right things.
- Behind procrastination often lies the fear of failure, the fear of success, or the fear of taking risks.
- To achieve what you want out of life you have to be willing to do things you don't really want to do.
- A priciple-based life results in self discipline.
- the reward of self-discipline is excellence.
- the byproduct of self-discipline is the ability to make a difficult task look easy.
- rest is as important a priority as work.

Building your strategy for Self-discipline

Is there an area in your life where you lack discipline? Ask yourself these three questions.

- **Why is it important to have self-discipline in this area?**

- **What benefits will self-discipline bring?**

- **What is your motivation for change?**

When you are convinced *why* you need this discipline develop your strategy to achieve it. Here are some steps to take.

1. Do some preliminary research in this area. (books, tapes, people)
2. Develop your plan and schedule it into your calendar. Set small, realistic goals.
3. Take about 15 minutes each morning to focus, prepare, and pray for this area.
4. If possible, tackle your discipline during a time of day when you have the most energy.
5. Find someone trustworthy to hold you accountable.
6. Build consistency in your discipline. Use a system that works for you.
7. Celebrate your breakthroughs.

Read, Reflect, & Respond

The following exercises are designed to help you identify any area that might hold you back from becoming self-disciplined.

Bible Study

Galatians 5:22-23 *But the fruit of the Spirit is love, joy, peace, patience, kindness, goodness, faithfulness, gentleness, self-control; against such things there is no law.*

Is there an area in your life where you lack the fruit of the Spirit? What are you doing to grow in this area?

Homework Questions

1. Reflect on a time in your past, or in the present, where a lack of discipline has cost you something tangible. What did you lose?
2. What fears keep you from achieving something specific you know the Lord has called you to do?

Small Group Questions

1. Is there a specific area of discipline you know you should tackle? Do you find yourself avoiding it?
2. What strategy will you use to develop this discipline? Who could hold you accountable?

Recommended Reading

The Disciplined Life: A Study in the Fine Art of Christian Discipleship, Richard Shelley Taylor (Beacon Hill Press: Kansas City, Missouri). A classic book on Christian discipleship.
The 21 Irrefutable Laws of Leadership, John C. Maxwell (Thomas Nelson Publishers: Nashville, Tennessee, 1998).

Chapter Six

♦ ♦ ♦

Developing People

Empower Others to Find Purpose

There is a loftier ambition than merely to stand high in the world. It is to stoop down and lift mankind a little higher.

—*Henry Van Dyke*

People Development
Empower Others to Find Purpose

Lord make me an instrument of your peace. Where there is hatred, let me show love; Where there is doubt—faith; where there is despair—hope; Where there is darkness—light; and where there is sadness—joy. Lord, grant that I may seek rather to comfort than to be comforted, to understand than to be understood, to love than to be loved. For it is by giving that one receives, by forgiving that one is forgiven, and by dying that one awakens to eternal life. Amen.

—St. Francis of Assisi

Commentary

To empower others to find purpose, consider two areas.

- First, understand **your own personality** and become secure in your identity. This will free you to believe the best about others and allow you to celebrate people's differences.
- Second, learn to **see people from God's perspective** and understand His unique design for them. Then you won't be tempted to judge them from your own limited view.

My First Lesson in Leadership

When I was a child, my sister used to call me John the Baptist. I was straight forward and, yes, blunt. Eager to get the job done I would often overlook people's feelings. It took me a while to realize that to get the job done I had to put people *first*.

A lesson in tact came one day in college. I had a roommate who slept in a bed that was never made, its covers buried under books and clothes. Her sprawled belongings covered practically every square inch of our room. *Squalor* was the best way I could describe it. How she ever managed to find anything in that disaster zone is still a mystery!

Enter Miss Pristine—that was me. If my roommate was one extreme, I was completely the other. Imagine anyone's irritation at trying to live in such a room. I tried my best to live with it, but my efforts were not very successful.

One day my patience ran out. Using the most diplomatic tone of my John the Baptist personality, I confronted my roommate about her need to pick up after herself—at *least* once in a while. The simple answer I received made a lasting impression on my life. She looked at me and said, "I won't receive that, because it wasn't said in love."

She was right. Case closed. So much for my attempt at diplomacy! I swallowed my pride and said nothing more.

Since that time I have worked hard to become more sensitive. While I may notice a need for improvement in others, I am slowly learning to "put on a heart of compassion, kindness, humility, gentleness, and patience" (Col. 3:12). It has improved my ability to work well with others. To be effective as a leader I had to learn to understand and value people.

Are You a Thinking or a Feeling Person?

There are two types of people in the world: those motivated by logic, and those by feelings. Feeling people have an innate ability to empathize and be sensitive to another's feelings. They take time to socialize before proceeding with the business at hand. Middle Easterners, for example, value building relationships before doing business and are superb hosts for that reason.

Most American business people are outcome oriented and are motivated more by logic than feelings. They want to cut to the chase. Chitchat is regarded as frivolous. That's why Americans who want to succeed in international business have to learn to tone down their directness and see the value of small talk.

It's true that women tend to be more sensitive than men but women can be process oriented too. Sensitive and direct personalities are both effective in relationships, but process-oriented women must invest more effort. The potential for misunderstanding increases when feeling and thinking people interact. They have to give room to the other and not jump to quick conclusions when something is communicated in a different style. That's why it is important to know your communication style and personality: It helps you become secure so you are free to appreciate the diversity in others.

75

If you've never taken a personality test and would like to, contact a local professional counseling service to request one. Most of them have those tools available. Understanding yourself will help you become more discerning and will make you a better listener. These are important leadership skills.

Take a minute to determine what motivates you. How does your orientation affect the way you relate to others? Consider the following:

- It's not enough to know your own style. You have to understand and respect the style that motivates others.
- The art of conversation is not simply saying the right thing at the right time. It's also knowing what to leave *unsaid* at the tempting moment.
- We often perceive others through the filters of our own experience and background.
- Prayer is a great way to understand another from God's perspective.

Model Leadership Qualities in Your Family

People management is not limited to a corporate environment. Most women, directly or indirectly, are in some form of management relationship with someone else. If you are a parent, your children are part of your management team. God has put them in your care for a season. Are you raising them to be godly leaders?

Although there are many benefits to information technology, it has created a bitter fragmentation in modern society. Many family members hardly know each other. Children live isolated, lonely lives, sitting for hours in front of their computers rather than in conversation with their parents. There is an absence of community.

Every day on the evening news there seems to be another report on how our youth are learning how to cope *without* parental supervision. Because children feel detached from their families many turn to the Internet to find online communities and chat rooms. These cyberspace relationships have become a substitute family. As comforting as these relationships may be, they are not adequate for building character and values.

To develop healthy leaders, begin in your own home. It takes more than a nuclear family to raise healthy children. The extended family of grandparents, aunts, uncles, in-laws, even close friends, plays an important role in your children's lives. That kind of family provides an environment for healthy feedback, modeling, balance, and security, which both adults and children need. If that has not been your experience as a family, look for ways to build those relationships. Develop simple traditions that encourage and nurture family members. Seek God's heart for each of your children, and affirm them in their potential. Encourage them to become purposeful, to learn from their mistakes, to take initiative, and to stand up for their convictions. Help them understand godly values, and be sure to live what you say. Then you will be able to raise children who are leaders.

The Story of a Survivor

One day my friend Billy was greeted at her door by a police officer announcing her husband's arrest. The reason? Bigamy! Could it be possible? As a traveling evangelist, Billy's husband married several wives and fathered many children all over the country.

Saddled under the shadow of humiliation, Billy suddenly found herself a single mother with two small boys to raise. What to do? Billy got on her knees and pleaded with the Lord for wisdom. She took the reigns of leadership and moved her family to Hawaii to join Youth With A Mission. There, God provided others to help Billy shoulder the full load of raising her children. Today, she and her sons lead healthy, productive lives because Billy was willing to *lead* her family through that difficult time of transition. Adversity has a way of bringing out the leader in us. Our response in times of crisis can leave a lasting impression on those who observe us.

Set a Different Standard

Friday nights were "movie nights" for most of my friends when I was growing up. Unfortunately, my mother did not allow our family to attend the theatre unsupervised. When I asked her why she replied, "Kathy, it's not necessary for you to follow the masses. If you lead a principled life, one day the masses will follow *you*!"

When John Kennedy Jr. wanted to pursue acting as a career his mother challenged him to be more purposeful by saying, "Do you want to portray others, or do you want others to portray you?" John took his mother's advice and pursued law instead. His early, tragic death left a nation longing for what could have been.

Here are five ways to nurture leadership attitudes in your children, and those in your circle of influence:

- **Model what you teach.** Behavioral scientists believe that modeling is the greatest determinant of human behavior. People will follow what you do far more than what you say.

- **Create an atmosphere of trust.** Real communication happens when people feel safe.

- **Encourage initiative.** Even if someone tries and fails, they'll learn *something* from the experience than if they never tried at all.

- **Identify principles.** When you take time to help others think through situations and identify important principles and truths you help them gain wisdom, insight and values.

- **Affirm people's gifts and potential.** There is nothing more reassuring than to be recognized by others for your gifts. Regardless of age people relish this affirmation.

How Jesus Developed People

People are every organization's greatest asset. The more people you develop the greater the extent of your dreams.[15] Leaders who do not work successfully with people will never rise to their leadership potential or influence. Because women are nurturers by nature, they often make better listeners and managers of people than men. Women bring rich gifts to the leadership arena. Our challenge is to accept and develop them so we can lead with confidence.

Jesus sets an excellent example for us of how to lead confidently and affirm the value of others. Here are some examples.

1. He gave people His undivided attention

In John 4 Jesus encounters the Samaritan woman at the well. As a Jew, He belonged to "the other side." Jews and Samaritans were not on speaking terms. Yet he broke that tradition to speak to this woman. It was the greatest affirmation she received in years!

Give your full attention when someone is speaking. It conveys that you value them as a person.

2. He was accessible to everyone—even children

Nicodemus was a Pharisee and a ruler of the Jews. He sought to see Jesus at night because he did not want others to see him asking spiritual questions. By the time he found him, Jesus was probably exhausted from a full day of demanding questions from his disciples and the crowds. He could have turned Nicodemus away. Instead, he chose to see him because he knew the man had a genuine need.

Brother Andrew, founder of Open Doors, a ministry to the persecuted church, often says that the simple act of *showing up* is the best affirmation you can give, especially if people realize you paid a price to be there. Being present during important moments makes people feel honored. It makes them know they are valued.

We affirm others by being available and accessible.

3. He saw people's hidden potential.

One day Jesus looked at Simon Peter and said, " and I also say to you that you are Peter, and upon this rock I will build my church; and the gates of Hades shall not overpower it. I will give you the keys of the kingdom of heaven; and whatever you shall bind on earth shall be bound in heaven, and whatever you shall loose on earth shall be loosed in heaven" (Matt. 16:18).

Who was Peter? A rough fisherman with a temper! One who denied Jesus three times when He was arrested. Jesus knew that Peter would one day mature to become an apostle of the church, but it would take *time*.

Leaders aren't created overnight. They develop over many years. It takes time to acquire the right foundation. Your input into people's lives is a part of a lifelong process of education. Like my college roommate, you may be in someone's life briefly yet are able to leave a lifelong impression. It's not the duration of the relationship that counts, but what transpires during the relationship.
One of the best ways to empower others is to affirm their potential even if it isn't evident at the time.

Successful people need to be affirmed too. After Debbie Boone won a Grammy Award for her song "You Light Up My Light" her music career took off like a rocket making her an instant international star. As a friend of the family, I met her during one of her tours. When I congratulated her and remarked about the platform that God had given her to be His witness, she was moved to tears. Since her success she had received mostly criticism from Christians. Together we prayed for protection and boldness for Debbie to be a powerful witness for the Lord. To this day, Debbie uses her celebrity status to be a light for Jesus and to share her faith in every sphere of her influence. *Words have great power to build up or to destroy!*

4. He demonstrated truth in practical ways.
One day the disciples were arguing who among them was the greatest. Knowing their hearts, Jesus took a child by his side and said to them, "Whoever receives this child in My name receives Me; and whoever receives Me receives Him who sent Me; for he who is least among you, this is the one who is great" (Luke 9:48).

Surprise!

5. He was discerning of every situation.
When Jesus confronted the rich, young ruler to "sell everything he possessed and distribute it to the poor…" he placed his finger on the controlling motive of this man's heart – greed. (Luke 18:22) Before this man could follow Jesus he had to give up his security in riches.
A leader must be discerning in every situation and respond appropriately.

For security reasons, I've learned to evaluate my audience and adjust my presentations accordingly. Once I was speaking to the leadership of a church about strategic mission work in Central Asia when I noticed a woman dressed in black in the audience. She wore an inverted cross commonly used by Satanists. Even as an outsider I knew this woman did not belong in this discussion. Others simply assumed she was invited to the confidential briefing. I quickly changed the tone of my material rather than take chances. When the church later looked into the matter, they confirmed that this woman was involved in witchcraft and had come on her own initiative.

6. He was a master of open-ended questions

- "What do you think, Simon? From whom do the kings of the earth take customs and taxes, from their sons or from strangers?" (Matt. 17:25)
- "The baptism of John was from what source, from heaven or from men?" (Matt. 21:25)
- "Who do the multitudes say that I am?" (Luke 9:18)

Having asked those questions, Jesus took the opportunity to affirm Peter by saying, "Flesh and blood has not revealed this to you, but my Father who is in heaven" (Matt. 16:17). *Asking open-ended questions affirms others because it conveys that you value their opinion.*

My friend Lee has an uncanny ability to do this. Whenever she is around my friends, I learn more about them because of the kinds of questions she asks. For example, when someone mentions her vocation most of us would say, "That's nice!" Not Lee. She says, "So you're a teacher? What class do you teach? How do you feel about trends in modern education? What is your opinion about how our current education system is affecting our youth?" Those open-ended questions cause people to talk about themselves. Once Lee learns about them, she can affirm and encourage them in the Lord.

Everyone needs and responds to encouragement!

Assess Your People Skills

You are always influencing others by your actions and words sometimes in ways that are totally oblivious to you. As a leader, the role you choose to play in people's lives is very important.

- Do you try to understand people by taking time to listen to them? It's very important to lead, encourage and lay out a vision for others, but the bottom line is acceptance. You have to help people find God's place for them not your place for them. Sometimes it is the same place. Sometimes it's not.[16]

- Do you know how to make people feel important? Every human being has this need. Good leaders know how to say the right words that bring out the best in people. Make a point every day to say and do things that build someone else's self esteem.

- Are you asking the right questions about people? Here are some of them.
  What are their strengths and are they using them?
  Do they have clear directions and expectations of their job?
  Am I giving them space to fail and learn from their own mistakes?
  Do they have ownership of the job and the vision?
  Am I spending enough time to develop this person?

- Am I willing to confront or manage conflict in a manner that brings positive outcomes? This is a task most leaders (especially women) least enjoy but one that cannot be overlooked. Conflict is a signal that a problem exists. Resolving conflict in a healthy way may lead to innovation and change. Sometimes better decision making and problem solving occurs under conflict. When a leader sees conflict as a positive force they can help make it a growing and positive experience for everyone. However there is a skill to doing this. Our next section provides some important insights for this skill.

Care Enough to Confront

Whenever humans come together, there is always the potential for conflict. It's what makes us unique! When conflict raises its ugly head you have to make a choice. Will you face it? Will you overlook it? Or will you deny it?

Many women would rather die than confront someone who has offended them or who is acting out of line. Perhaps it's because women often equate confrontation with rejection. It's impossible to grow and mature if we are only willing to receive positive input from others and discredit feedback that challenges our behavior. A leader must first learn to *receive* correction before they are able to effectively *give* correction to others.

You will discover in your role as a leader that some battles must be engaged, and you are the one called on to do it. There's the rub! How do you get your point across so it is heard but doesn't decimate the hearer? I've been in situations where the person confronting was so diplomatic that their concerns came across as an affirmation rather than a challenge. In response, the hearer thanked them for the compliment and walked away. Have you done that? I know I have. It doesn't do the job, does it? Then you have to confront the person again and say, "Remember that compliment I gave you the other day? It was actually meant to be a challenge. Let me put it another way..."

If you feel you need coaching on how to confront, I recommend you read the book *Caring Enough to Confront* by David Augsburg.[17] It is an excellent resource that has helped many develop skills in this area.

Few people enjoy confronting others but it can be done in a positive manner. John Maxwell lists ten keys to remember when you confront others. They are biblical principles that will help you have the right attitude and approach in such situations. Here they are:

The Ten Commandments of Confrontation[18]

1. Do it privately, not publicly.

2. Do it as soon as possible. It's more natural than waiting a long time.

3. Speak to one issue at a time.

4. Once you've made your point don't keep repeating it.

5. Deal only with actions the person can change.

6. Avoid sarcasm. It signals you are angry and you'll lose credibility.

7. Avoid words like *always* and *never.* They make people defensive.

8. Present criticism as suggestions or questions if possible.

9. Don't apologize for the confrontational meeting. Doing so may indicate you aren't sure you have the right to say what you did.

10. Don't forget to compliment the person at the beginning and the end.

Styles in Conflict Resolution

We each respond to interpersonal conflict in different ways. Our style is sometimes influenced by the way our family handled conflict. You can either emulate that style or react against it and take an opposite stance. People who were raised in an abusing family situation will often shun conflict of any kind because it holds painful memories. Some women use manipulation to manage their way out of difficult situations. It worked with their mothers so they do it too!

There are many ways people respond to interpersonal conflict. Here are some of them. Can you identify your style?

1. **The Avoidance Style** is a decision to let the conflict work out by itself. It is a subconscious aversion to tension and frustration. It is a passive style that may send the signal that you don't care. Nevertheless it can be useful if a conscious decision is made to use it as the most appropriate response for the situation. For example if two people are venting out a problem that does not concern you or the company. Don't get involved, just listen.

2. **The Forcing Style** involves abuse of power and dominance. It is an uncooperative "win-lose" approach where only one person wins. Forcing is not useful in long-term relationships and brings an unfavorable response from others.

3. **The Accommodating Style** represents behavior that is cooperative but not assertive. It is a passive act that can be perceived as weak. In many cultures this is a commonly accepted style. It is useful when an individual you work with (i.e. boss) abuses their power towards you.

4. **The Compromising Style** represents behavior that is between cooperative and assertive. It's a give and take process and can involve negotiation and a series of concessions. However compared to the collaborative style, it does not maximize joint outcomes.

5. **The Collaborative Style** is definitely the "win-win" approach where both parties win. This style represents a desire to maximize joint outcomes. People who use this style see conflict as a natural process that leads to helpful, creative solutions. They respect others as equals with legitimate opinions. A team approach in your management style accommodates this conflict solution style most of the time.[19] This approach is also useful when resolving conflict in marriage.

Some Questions to Ponder

How effective are you in navigating conflict? What style do you use? Ask these questions to determine your effectiveness:

1. What is God's perspective on the situation? (Stay objective)
2. What is the real issue? (Focus on the problem, not the person)
3. Is this a blind spot for them? (If so, they'll need instruction)
4. Are they intentionally acting this way? (If so, they'll need to be challenged)
5. Does the Lord want me to challenge them? (Be sure you are the right person)

Finally, consider humor to help you get your point across in a potentially tense situation. Good humor can be a powerful tool. It endears you to others. Here is how one woman manager used humor to challenge her boss.

The CEO of a home furnishing company hired Angela to oversee his Accessories Purchasing Department. It wasn't long before she discovered that this man had a *passion* for trinkets. Without consulting her, he made poor purchasing decisions that affected the company and her department. When one of his orders completely failed to attract customers, Angela, as the manager, had to find a creative way to challenge her boss. One morning she entered his office and said, "Why don't we offer the sweater shavers free with the purchase of one of our flannel sheet sets?" The CEO laughed when he realized he was responsible for purchasing too many sweater shavers. He quickly got the message. From that day forward, he left the buying decisions to his purchasing manager.

Summary

Empowering others to become purposeful is a leadership responsibility. To do that, keep in mind the following:

- Understand your own personality.
- Learn to see people from God's perspective by praying for them.
- Recognize your team is comprised of those in your immediate circle of influence.
- Affirm others by:
  - Giving them your undivided attention when they speak to you
  - Being accessible
  - Recognizing their hidden potential
  - Asking open-ended questions
  - Being available as a mentor

- Be solution oriented during times of conflict.

Building A Strategy
For Developing People

Who are the people you are developing? How would you fair if you asked them to rate you as a leader using the methods Jesus used to develop people? Here are some examples –

- He made them feel important by listening to them.
- He was accessible when they had a genuine need.
- He saw and affirmed people's hidden potential.
- He shared practical principles.
- He discerned and addressed their real needs.
- He created a safe environment for open communication.
- He always confronted in love.

PEOPLE DEVELOPMENT

If you know you fall short in an area of people management, build a plan to help you grow in this area. Consider these suggestions –

Study someone who is a good role model to inspire you in this area.
Set specific goals each day to encourage you to initiate new behaviors.
Develop questions to use that help you connect better with others.
Pray regularly for others and ask God to give you His heart for them.

Your daily routine holds the keys to your success!

Read, Reflect, & Respond

The following exercises are designed to help you identify your strengths and weaknesses in developing people.

Bible Study

Take a few minutes alone to read and reflect on the following Scripture.

- Matthew 7:21 *"Not everyone who says to Me, Lord, Lord, will enter the kingdom of heaven; but he who does the will of My Father who is in heaven."*
  What principles was Jesus teaching in this saying? How does it relate to developing leaders?

Homework Questions

1. List a couple of ways you plan to affirm someone you are developing?

2. Think of a time when you were able to resolve a conflict with another person in a way that brought honor to God? Why was it successful? What did you learn from the experience?

Small Group Questions

When was the last time you had to confront someone or resolve conflict? What style of conflict resolution did you use? How successful was it? Would you do anything different next time?

Recommended Reading

Caring Enough to Confront, David Augsburg, (Augsburg Press: Lynnwood, Washington). A classic book on conflict resolution.
Mary Kay on People Management, Mary Kay Ash (Warner Books, a division of Time Warner Company: New York, 1984). An excellent book on the art of managing and affirming people on your team.
The Survivor Personality, Al Siebert (Practical Psychology Press: Portland, Oregon, 1994). A psychiatrist explores strategies on how to deal with difficult people and gain strength from adversity.

Chapter Seven

◆ ◆ ◆

Opposites Do Not Always Attract

Follow God's Purpose in a Man's World

The current feminist agenda mostly accuses men or society in general, thereby ignoring the pivotal role played by women themselves in their life predicaments. Let's face it: There is no destiny outside of what you give up or take on.

—Dr. Laura Schlessinger

Opposites Do Not Always Attract
Follow God's Purpose in a Man's World

Lord let my affirmation come from the knowledge that I am accepted by You, empowered by Your wisdom and Spirit and sent out to bless others in Your name. Amen.

Commentary

Carmen was an educated, highly intelligent, and capable young woman. When she was overlooked for a leadership position in her company, for which she was qualified, I was surprised. In a conversation with the company president, I casually inquired why Carmen was not chosen. He explained, "Oh, she is a bright and capable woman, but she doesn't command the men's respect as a leader. I'm afraid they will not accept her in this position."

Carmen *had* the skills for the job. What she lacked was an understanding of the leadership *culture*. In that company, leaders were expected to be direct and brief in their communication. Carmen tended to be longwinded and indirect. She also dressed rather flamboyantly in a manner that drew more attention to her clothing style rather than to her person. She had the skills but lacked the "presence" or "image" for the job. So Carmen was overlooked for the position.

This chapter attempts to address sensitive issues that frequently surface when men and women work together. It is not meant to discredit men, but to help women understand the leadership culture in which they serve.

Finding the Balance

Throughout history women have struggled to find their place in leadership circles. Yes, we've had female superstars in every era – Esther, Deborah, Florence Nightingale, and so on but they've been the exception not the rule. If one woman can do it why can't more? Perhaps its because societies and cultures have not allowed room for too many women to rise to a place of prominence.

The good news we are living in a new day! Today God is providing women fresh opportunity to influence their communities, their society, their nation and the world at large. I don't believe God had a change of heart. He always said, "it was not good for man to be alone." The job was too much for the man to carry out single-handedly. That's why He gave the cultural mandate to both Adam *and* Eve. It would require both of them, walking and working together to carry it out.

Today, practically every nation of the world is experiencing some form of leadership crisis. Whenever I'm in another country I make it a point to read the English version of the local newspaper. Without exception, every newspaper I've read in the last few years – in Israel, Turkey, Kyrghyzstan, England, Australia, all seem to report a crisis in leadership in their country. The people don't believe their leaders have the necessary insight to lead their nation into the future.

God has given His Church that wisdom. He wants discerning men and women to team up and lead from their respective strengths. For that to happen, women must stop trying to lead using a masculine approach. They need to lead from the rich gifts God has put within them. They need to allow these gifts to rise and find mature expression – gifts of discernment, personal warmth, creativity and patience. Today it's thrilling to see women, from practically every country, are sensing God's call to step out and provide compassionate and creative leadership in their communities. The book, *Women as Risk Takers for God*, is an excellent documentary on this subject. The world is crying out for more men *and* women to provide leadership in places of great need and opportunity.

Honor God's Order

Leadership has its joys and privileges. It also has its challenges and responsibilities. As a woman leader, your first responsibility is to develop a clear sense of God's order for your life. Just because you've heard the call of God does not mean you are expected to step out immediately. God is looking for a willing heart that responds with a resounding yes! Like Joseph, sometimes it takes years of training and preparation before you are released. Make sure you understand your priorities – God first, family second, and service third!

Priority 1: Keep God First in Your Relationships

Leadership begins with Christ. Your submission to the Lord and His leadership prepares you to rightly represent Him in life and service. Before you can do anything *for* Him, you have to *know* Him. You have to experience His companionship and learn His ways.

Priority 2: Respect Your Husband

If you are married, your husband is your second priority. "For the husband is the head of the wife, as Christ also is the head of the church" (Eph. 5:22). Learn to honor and respect him. Allow God to work in both of you as a couple. Pray daily for your husband. Look for ways to encourage and build him up. Never build your career or ministry at the expense of your marriage. The quality of a leader is often reflected in the quality of his or her marriage.

Priority 3: Nurture Your Children

"Children, obey your parents in the Lord, for this is right. Honor your father and mother, which is the first commandment with a promise" (Eph. 6:1–2). There is no contest. Honoring your parents is God's commandment, not a suggestion. Make it easy for your child to honor you by providing godly counsel, training, and nurture. Parents who schedule uninterrupted time with their children, listen to their questions, and have fun with them will reap rich rewards.

Priority 4: Commit to Service

When the above priorities are established in your life, the foundation is set for you to answer your call to service. That foundation prevents your husband from feeling he is in competition with your ministry, or your children resenting those to whom you minister.

Every woman, whether single or married, will one day stand before God to give an account for her life. How have you used your gifts and talents? How have you honored God during your lifetime? Wouldn't it be a shame to realize at that moment that you missed out on God's purpose because you didn't understand His order or have the courage to follow His call?

Know Your Leadership Style

Have you ever wondered why some people are always treated special, whether they are in a department store, a bank, a restaurant or just mingling around with people at a party? Behavioral experts say that these people possess a quality known as "Altic Presence." Sometimes it's called "chutzpah" which in Yiddish means assertiveness. These people know their strengths and cultivate them. They exhibit confidence when facing new experiences. They refuse to be intimidated. Regardless of their circumstances, regardless of who's confronting them, people with chutzpah consider themselves equal to everyone else and expect to be treated with equal respect.[20]

This confidence can be learned but at the heart of chutzpah is an understanding and acceptance of one's own strengths and gifts. Leaders are made not born. As you establish God's order in your life take time to discover your leadership style. Finding your unique expression is very rewarding and will help you build confidence and chutzpah! According to Machiavelli, author of *The Prince,* leadership styles fall roughly into four categories that apply to both men and women.[21] See if you can identify yours.

The Commanding Leader

This one wants control. She is a take-charge kind of person who gets things done and expects others to take direction from her.

In her role as the first woman of Great Britain, Prime Minister Margaret Thatcher demonstrated this type of leadership. During Britain's war in the Falkland Islands she spoke decisively about Britain's objectives for the war and assured her countrymen and the world that the operation would succeed. She carried out her role with confidence, without losing her femininity.

THE COMMANDING LEADER

- Focuses on control
- Is a take-charge person
- Achieves results
- Persuades by directing
- Rapidly changes

The Logical Leader

This type prefers to use reason to achieve her objectives. She is more analytical. She persuades by walking people through their reasoning.

Queen Esther used logic to appeal to the king, showing him factually who his true enemies were. She used logical persuasion to build her case—and won.

THE LOGICAL LEADER

- Analyzes new directions
- Solves complex problems
- Formulates plans
- Persuades by reasoning
- Introduces change incrementally

OPPOSITES DO NOT ALWAYS ATTRACT

The Inspirational Leader

This is a creative person who empowers others by inviting them to share in her vision.

Mother Theresa was a renowned inspirational leader. She recruited thousands of men and women to serve with the Sisters of Charity among the world's poor. She became a voice for the poor through writing, speaking, and media events.

THE INSPIRATIONAL LEADER

- Envisions new opportunities
- Introduces radical ideas
- Empowers others
- Persuades by creating trust
- Invokes radical change

The Supportive Leader

She prefers the power of connections with others, rather than the more direct, controlling approach. She wants to involve other people in the decision-making process. She seeks consensus.

During her husband's campaign for the presidency, Elizabeth Dole took an active role and spoke to audiences herself. Many of her presentations were delivered not from behind the podium, but by walking around the room and personally connecting with her audience. As president of the Red Cross she skillfully recruited funds and volunteers to this organization by creating practical opportunities for people to become involved.

THE SUPPORTIVE LEADER

- Tries for consensus
- Facilitates work
- Encourages openness
- Persuades by involving
- Introduces reactive change

Which of these styles do you believe reflects your leadership expression? Ask others who work with you or know you well for their feedback. The way you know your style is that it leaves you feeling fulfilled and energized. Finding your style will help you better use your strengths and appreciate differences in the style of others. As you develop your style you will grow in confidence as a leader.

Women in Leadership

The moment you assume a leadership role you bring to that function your strengths and weaknesses. As you mature, you are able to execute the role with wisdom and grace. In any endeavor that's new it's natural to feel unsure at first. Expect to make mistakes. Practice doesn't make perfect, nor is it supposed to. Practice is about increasing your repertoire of ways to recover from your mistakes.[22] As the adage goes, "Nothing ventured, nothing gained." An immature leader will have a tendency to exhibit the following behaviors:

- Controlling others
- Failing to delegate
- Making your leadership role your identity
- Showing overt favoritism
- Rescuing others from their mistakes

It's one thing to lead among those who recognize and affirm your leadership. It's quite another to stand confidently when your authority is questioned. That's the acid test of leadership. That's the test many women in leadership must be prepared to face.

Discrimination can come from both men and women in subtle and overt ways. The subtle form comes in ways you can't see, feel, or touch, but it still leaves you feeling undermined, insulted, ignored, patronized, and/or excluded. It's as though you are invisible in some meetings.

The overt form includes being overlooked for a promotion in spite of competence and commitment, or receiving less compensation than people with similar positions. It can include being interrupted in midsentence, having your input met with total silence, then watching the conversation continue in a different vein. Talented, intelligent, educated women in ministry circles as well as in business live and work daily under such conditions. What should be their response?

If you are experiencing such challenges, I recommend finding a mature, godly woman who can mentor and nurture you through it. As you work with that person, ask "Where is God in all of this?" This is a healthy way to work through your emotions so you aren't tempted to resort to behaviors that ultimately undermine your leadership authority and credibility. A leader is first and foremost a problem solver. You have to begin by solving your own problems before you can expect to lead others through theirs.

Women need to remember that unmet needs or hurts from the past can dictate the way you relate to men. They may cause you to fall into a stereotype that sabotages your leadership success. Here is what some of those roles are like.

The Superwoman
She tries to please and gain male affirmation by over committing and not delegating. She thinks her hard work will be appreciated, but in the end she usually feels used and resentful. (Some people will take advantage of her work and ideas to enhance their own position and neglect to give her credit.)

The Cheerleader
Overly agreeable and compliant, she acts cute and cheerful no matter how she feels. Frequently these women will put their leader or pastor on a pedestal, idolizing them. This comes out of a need for a father's affirmation and affection. (Men enjoy and are flattered by her because she makes them feel good, but in their minds, she's not a leader.)

The Iron Maiden
She tends to be 'business only', and is often aggressive, cold, unapproachable, and lacking a sense of humor. Her work is her identity. Behind her stern exterior often lies a fear of male rejection or a firm decision to protect against being hurt.

The Mother/Counselor
She is always holding men's hands and giving them advice, acting as a sounding board, nurturing them when they feel insecure. She has a need to be needed, and this is one way she may win her way into men's hearts.

The Seductress
She uses sexuality in her manner and dress to manipulate men's attention and get her way. This woman often has a rebellious nature, does not like to play by the rules, and looks for shortcuts to get what she wants.

Women who want to become mature leaders need to avoid the temptation to fall into those roles. Promotion comes from God. He lifts women up as He promises in Psalm 75:6–7: "For not from the east, nor from the west, nor from the desert comes exultation. But God is the Judge. He puts down one, and exalts another."

The Differences of a "Man's World"

God wants men and women to celebrate their differences. In order to do so they must learn to understand each other, especially their work, communication styles *and* their culture.

There is a male culture, a female culture and a mixed gender culture. The rule is that the majority rules. In a predominantly male team the male culture rules. In a predominantly female team the female culture rules unless the leader is a man. In a mixed culture the rules are divided between both cultures.

OPPOSITES DO NOT ALWAYS ATTRACT

At the executive level of any organization there is also *a leadership culture*. It also has it's own unspoken rules. Failure to understand them can limit your career. Heed its rules and watch your credibility grow! Here are some keys to help you fit well in a leadership culture:

1. Communicate Concisely

The *way* we communicate conveys meaning. In general, men use conversation to gain information while women use conversation to interact. Men want the facts. Women value relationships and want to connect. With those differences in mind, women need to remember to keep their communication with men concise and brief. Men aren't interested in all the details. Elaborate descriptions are a quick way to lose their interest. Stick to the essentials and cut out the flowery adjectives. If you tend to be wordy, try to rehearse your communication before you speak. Look for ways to abbreviate. Men will respect you more as a leader and be more attentive to what you have to say.

Here are some examples:
a. WEAK: "This solution appears to be viable and one you will find interesting."
   REVISED: "I think this solution will work."
b. WEAK: "With hard work and time we can expect that our plans will merge well together."
   REVISED: "We expect a good fit."
c. WEAK: "We have worked hard at many options and believe we now have a good solution."
   REVISED: We have a solution."

2. Regain the Floor

You're the only woman on the team. The meeting becomes heated, and you have an excellent solution to the issue at hand. Your input is ignored or even interrupted while the men go on talking as though you were not in the room. What do you do?

At this point, many women tend to assume a silent-observer position, wondering *Why in the world am I even in this group?* Silent retreats only perpetuate the problem. In reality, a number of things could be going on:

- You spoke so softly some of the men didn't even hear you.
- You took too long to get to the point and they became impatient.
- You were out of sync with the dynamics of the meeting.

Over the years, I've served on at least ten different boards. (Thank goodness the Lord is beginning to cure me of that illness!) In most cases I was the only woman on the team. It took time for some men to accept me as a peer. I learned to be patient. Here is what I recommend if you are in a similar situation.

- Ask God to give you His wisdom for each meeting.
- Do your homework. Read the minutes/reports and come prepared with ideas.
- Dress professionally and be immaculately groomed.
- Arrive on time, and make sure you personally greet every member.
- Always have a positive attitude towards everyone.
- Be attentive, take notes, and try to understand the issue being discussed.
- Present your comments concisely in a clear voice. If your comments are overlooked and you believe your contribution is important, repeat your comment and ask a question that requires a response.
- Expect to make a positive contribution.

3. Don't Be Too Accessible

From youth, women are raised to serve others. As leaders, they tend to be relational and considerate of people's feelings. A servant leader affirms the value and worth of others.

However, an overly accessible leader wastes her valuable time and robs people of the opportunity to figure things out for themselves. She sends the message that she doesn't have enough important work to do and she doesn't value her own priorities enough to be selectively accessible.

Learning to say no is a powerful leadership principle. It frees you to be available for those opportunities that will bring the best return, and it increases your credibility as a leader.

4. Guard Your Privacy

As a rule, you don't hear men blithely discussing health problems or a recent run-in with their mother-in-law. Men usually keep private matters to themselves.

Women, too, must do the same if they want respect. If you're having one of those bad PMS days, keep it to yourself. And whatever you do, never cry in a professional setting. That sends the message that you're too emotional to lead. In a man's world, leaders don't cry. Neither do they complain or seek sympathy and understanding. They stand tall and face each challenge with courage. You must do the same.

5. Conviction and Energy

In spite of his advanced age, Ronald Reagan lived his presidency with such energy and conviction that even his opponents loved him. He definitely had chutzpah! People admired his humor, his enthusiasm, and his quiet confidence, even when they disagreed with his policies or felt he was operating outside his expertise. His energy and enthusiasm endeared him to his public.

Leaders with low energy convey a lack of stamina. Women are sometimes at a disadvantage, especially if they have a soft voice or are small in stature. I've met women almost six feet tall who spoke so softly you could hardly understand them over regular office noise. I've also seen tiny women overcompensate by literally shouting when they speak in front of a group. If you want to project authority, keep *passion* in your voice, not loudness.

Eight Ways to be Included in Your Leadership Network

Some women leaders never seem to be invited to the formal and informal social functions of their leadership team. Breaking into areas of influence traditionally dominated by men is possible, but challenging. Some organizations allow entry into this network based on merit or exchange value. Others have high standards *and* insist on being male as the criteria. Many women are not necessarily excluded from this network but are blocked from knowing important information such as what plans are in the making, new job openings and personal developments in other leaders lives. *Information is influence!*

If you find yourself challenged in this area here are eight keys that might help.

Eight Ways to be Included in a Leadership Network[23]

1. Demonstrate self-confidence and initiative.
2. Acquire behaviors and traits of successful leaders (savvy of the informal organization, knowing the Big Picture, being a direct communicator, flexibility, problem solving, being a team member, knowing politics, and so on.)
3. Know your organization from top to bottom (how it works, how things get done, how it's organized, strategic plans, etc.)
4. Personally know as many of the "movers and shakers" as you can.
5. Establish multiple reciprocal networks with others (it's effective because some of these individuals may get promoted to the top.)
6. Get spiritual and moral support from informal women's groups.
7. Get involved in high visibility projects where your gifts can be seen. Don't hide your gift under a bushel!
8. Become indispensable in the success of key projects not just in technical expertise but also by having a good sense of humor and good people skills that make others enjoy working with you.

One female secretary stayed late listening to her boss's negotiations with clients. She critiqued the contracts and then compared her notes with her boss's to see if she was on target. One day her boss sighted upon one of her marked-up contracts and was genuinely impressed by her insights. He handed her a life-changing note of confidence: Night-school tuition to get a business degree. Today, she owns her own company and is a very successful and wealthy women. In 1999 she received Microsoft's Best E-commerce Solution award.[24]

Most women will find entry into a leadership network when the network members see them as competent, with a potential to contribute to the group.

Be Wise

Women often underestimate how easily men are aroused by the opposite sex. Subtle gestures like standing too close to a man, whispering in his ear, touching, or an innocent hug can send a different message than what was intended. The rule of thumb is always to dress and act professionally in the workplace; keep clothes, jewelry, and makeup toned down; and keep your hands to yourself. Men will respect you as you act with modesty and high personal standards.

Here are some guidelines to help you act discretely around male associates. These are sensitive issues, but important to note.

1. Avoid traveling long distances alone with a man who is not your spouse or brother. If you have no choice, sit in a different row to create some distance. Demanding travel schedules can put coworkers in vulnerable situations.
2. If a man is acting too friendly let him know you are uncomfortable with his behavior. Find ways to avoid being alone with him. If he is your boss and you have little control over the situation, find another job. The price of staying isn't worth it.
3. As much as possible, avoid working alone with a man for long hours at night. It's best to avoid situations that lead to temptation or give even the appearance of evil.
4. Don't offer a sympathetic ear to a man who has marital problems or who is recently divorced. Keep your distance from men who might be in vulnerable situations.
5. Keep your hands to yourself. Your innocent hug or pat on the shoulder may send a different signal than you intended to a man. Most men are very sensitive to touch.

Summary

Working in a man's world can be demanding and also rewarding, especially when you learn how to play by the rules. Recognize that men have much to teach you too.

Women bring unique gifts and insights into every leadership team. They can be intuitive and discerning, often perceiving important subtleties that make a big difference in the success of a venture. Never apologize for being a woman, but be discrete and appropriate. Walk in God's authority and wisdom.

I believe that some of the best leaders in this new millennium will be women. Maybe that's because we've finally heard enough success stories to believe that women actually can lead. Maybe it's because God has ordained it that way. Maybe it's because this is our hour!

In this chapter you have reviewed:

- Put this order in your life - God first, family second and service third.
- To gain confidence as a leader, know and develop your leadership style.
- Don't allow yourself to be intimidated by discrimination.
- Continue to demonstrate competence, effectiveness, productivity, and the ability to advance. These will help you be noticed as a person with leadership ability.
- Use discretion when working with men so that you don't become a stumbling block for anyone.

Building Your Strategy
for Working in a Leadership Culture

When I was growing up my mother always reminded me to "be appropriate in every situation." Ask yourself these questions:

- Presently, which culture am I called to serve? (Male, female, mixed, leadership?)
- What are the unspoken rules of this culture?
- Am I functioning "appropriately" in this culture? Do I make a valuable contribution?
- Am I serving from a pure heart – caring for the needs of others not just my own.
- Where can I be growing so I can be more valuable to this team?
- What action plan will I take to grow in this direction?

Continued success is a result of continued improvement.[25]

Read, Reflect, & Respond

The following questions are designed to help you evaluate your behavior and performance around male co-workers.

Bible Study

Take a few minutes alone to read and reflect on the following Scripture. Record your thoughts in a journal.

Matthew 10:16 *Behold, I send you as sheep in the midst of wolves; therefore be as wise as serpents and as innocent as doves.*
How are you keeping your thoughts and ways pure with the men you work for or with? Are you experiencing a struggle or temptation?

Homework Questions

Is there a situation in your life when your behavior towards a man — either a spouse, a boss, or a co-worker—turned out poorly. How did you respond? What did you learn? What would you do differently next time?

Small Group Question

We learn most of our interpersonal skills from watching our parents. How has your relationship with your father (or another significant man in your life) influenced your perception of men today?

Recommended Reading

The Articulate Executive: Learn to Look, Act, and Sound Like a Leader, Grandville N. Toogood, (MCGraw-Hill: New York, 1996) An excellent resource to help you learn to communicate effectively.
Women at the Crossroads, Kari Torjesen Malcolm (InterVarsity Press: Downers Grove, Illinois, 1982) Explores the biblical role of women.
They Don't Get It, Do They? Kathleen Kelly Reardon (Little, Brown and Company: New York, 1993). This book deals with how a woman can gain credibility in the corporate world, and the challenges she'll face getting it.
Women As Risktakers for God, Lorry Lutz (Baker Books: Grand Rapids, Michigan, 1998).

Read, Reflect & Respond

Chapter Eight

Something to Die For

Discover God's Heart and Purpose for the World

There are no precedents on record for the harvest of souls—the number of people coming to Christ and into fellowship with c h u r c h e s — n o w occurring daily all over the world. We are in the midst of the greatest prayer movement that could ever have been imagined.

—*C. Peter Wagner*

Something to Die For
Discover God's Heart and Purpose for the World

Lord give me a heart for the lost. Show me my place in Your great harvest. Teach me how I can be a blessing to the peoples of the earth so that the 'kingdom of the world becomes the kingdom of our Lord, and of His Christ.' Amen.

Commentary

Katya held her breath with excitement as she opened the little black box. There, enveloped in black velvet, was an exquisite pair of emerald earrings. "These are for you," the hostess said. Katya was speechless. All her life she dreamt of owning a pair of emerald earrings. Now they were hers. How could a stranger offer her such an expensive gift? The answer was simple: The stranger was a Christian sharing God's love with an atheist.

This was Katya's first visit to the US. In fact, it was her first trip outside her homeland, Turkmenistan. As an educator she was looking forward to using her visit to research teaching methods. Finding God was not in her plans. A simple act of hospitality and generosity opened Katya's heart to the Lord. Led by the Holy Spirit, the Christian host planted the seeds of the gospel and, in time, Katya found the Lord. She returned to Turkmenistan to bring God's message of hope to her people.

That is a true story. It shows how God used the simple act of hospitality to take the gospel to a Muslim nation. Opportunities abound to bless people with simple acts of love. Most of the time we aren't aware of their significance. And we might never see the fruit of our obedience. That's not important. What matters is that we give God our resounding yes and join Him in His adventure.

God's Heart and Plan for the World

By now you know that to find your purpose you must begin with God. His desire for you is that you know Him and delight in His fellowship. What you are is God's gift to you. What you become is your gift to *Him*. Your responsibility is to develop your potential so that you become the person He intended you to be. Self-discipline is important, but there is more. Open your eyes to the new horizon that lets you see God's heart for the world. Now, let's explore how you do that.

What is God's heart and plan for the world? The blessing of *salvation*. It began with a promise God gave to Abraham, that through him and his family He would bless all the peoples of the earth. The Old Testament reveals how God worked through the people of Israel to carry out His promise. And even though Israel was called to be "a light to the nations" (Isa. 42:1–4), she failed to carry out His mandate. Therefore, the blessing was fulfilled when Jesus Christ came and sacrificed His life. God's plan for the world is to offer the blessing, the gift, of salvation.

History is not a series of random events. It shows His plan to bless all the families of the earth through His church, of which you, if you know Him, are a member. Your responsibility as a leader is to be available for God's purpose.

The Role of Women in God's Plan

In practically every culture of the world, women have played an important role in shaping their societies. Studies over the last ten years show that the influence goes beyond the community and social development, to spiritual transformation. In this generation women all over the world are playing an important role as *recipients* of the gospel and as *messengers* of the gospel. Consider these examples.

- Of the 260,000 Christians in Hong Kong, 60 percent are women.
- In one county in China, 83 percent of Christians are women.
- In Korea the gospel came first to the women. They were willing to read the Bible in the new simplified Korean script, but men refused to read it except in Chinese characters.
- The first Hottentot convert in Africa was a woman named Eva. The first Nazarene convert in Swaziland was Ruth, the lower wife of an old man.

- In China the house-church movement has grown largely through the ministry of uneducated women evangelists.
- In Japan the missionary wives are often the initial church planters, *after* which men move into traditional leadership roles.
- Of the 50,000 prayer cells in Paul Cho's church in Korea, only 3,000 of the leaders are men.
- The history of Europe contains stories of kings who became Christians as a result of their wives or mothers, including Vladamir, king of the Rus; and Ethelbert, king of Kent.
- In a study of converts from Islam in the United States, all of the women converts received the gospel from another woman or from a couple.
- During the early part of this century, the women's missionary movement in the United States involved more than 3 million women in 40 different denominational mission societies. This movement supported 2,500 missionaries and more than 6,000 indigenous women who ministered in 3,6000 schools, 80 hospitals, and 11 colleges.[26]

What Does It Mean?

Dr. Bryant Myer of MARC, World Vision, suggests that these statistics indicate that women are responsive to the gospel and are a receptive entry point to resistant peoples. He also suggests that women are the most likely to speak to unreached women and present the gospel in ways they understand. Women share a common heart language, which may mean that they will communicate the gospel more effectively in terms other women can understand.

As you stay open to the leading of the Holy Spirit expect Him to use you to reach other women. It could be through hospitality, as in the story with Katya. It could be through a program in your church. It could be as you befriend an international student. The opportunities are endless.

Like Queen Esther, God has uniquely designed you to make a difference. You will discover it when you acknowledge Him as the initiator of history. Your role is not to do things *for* God. Rather, it is to step back and *follow* Him in what He is doing. That's the fun of the adventure. It is an attitude of being available to the Holy Spirit to use you to bless others. It also requires that you develop interests outside yourself so you can understand, and lead others to understand, how the Lord is working in the world.

Find Your Place in God's Harvest

A team of Christian counselors who lived on the Big Island of Hawaii experienced remarkable results in their counseling practice. Soon, word of their success spread throughout the island. The Department of Social Services was impressed by the reports and was curious to meet the team. In a conversation with one of them, the director of Social Services said, "Years from now, I may not remember the content of our conversation, but I will never forget how I felt being in your presence."

What this man was experiencing was a taste of God's presence and glory. The counselor was not an exceptional person. She did not have an arresting personality or impressive academic credentials. What she did have was the wisdom to daily step aside and make room for God's presence in her life.

As you daily invite the Lord to rule in your life, you become a vessel for His presence and glory. As a result, wherever you go, whatever you do, you will leave behind the fragrance of His presence, a touch of His glory. As others experience it they will be drawn to the Lord.

Yielding your life to the Lord is committing yourself to His purpose. He will begin to open your eyes to His workings in the world. Over time, you will find yourself drawn to the role He intends—His purpose for you.

Here are some ways you can prepare yourself for your role:

Prayer is the first place you should go to find God's heart. How? What should you pray about?" The answer is simple. Learn to pray by praying. Try the following:

- Read about a nation or a people. Then take time to regularly pray for them. For information on various nations contact:

  a. The Global Prayer Digest
     U.S. Center for World Mission
     Web Address: www.USCWM.org
     phone: (626) 398-2249.

  b. Or read *Operation World: A Day-to-Day Guide to Praying for the World* by Patrick Johnstone (Zondervan Publishing House: Grand Rapids, Michigan, 1998).

- Join a mission prayer group in your church and pray with others about a nation.
- Join a group journey team that prayers on-sight in a neighborhood or country.

Intercession is the commitment to pray for a situation or person until the breakthrough comes. The Lord will show you how to pray so that you join Him in what He wants to accomplish in that situation. You may not see the results right away, but if you pray faithfully, in time, the fruit of your prayers will become evident.

Support Those Who Go

Susan was a journalist by training. She also was diagnosed with multiple sclerosis, which prevented her from traveling abroad. But that did not stop Susan from becoming deeply involved in her church's commitment to a Muslim nation.

While others on her team traveled and worked in the target country Susan kept the vision alive at home by using her writing skills. She did not allow her "disability" to hinder her from making a difference with her life.

You may never be called to be a missionary, yet your prayers, encouragement, and financial support of those on short- or long-term service are crucial. Ask the Lord to show you if you should adopt a missionary. If you don't know one, contact a local mission organization. You don't have to be a missionary to be mission-minded!

Offer Hospitality

It is said that at least 60 percent of the world's future leaders will, at some point in their lives, study in the US. Think about that! When you befriend an international student, you may be meeting someone who could one day become a leader in their nation. International-student ministries are frequently looking for host homes. Open your home during the holidays and invite foreign guests to experience Christian hospitality. Inquire at your local university to see if they have visiting scholars. If your neighbors are immigrants, extend a warm welcome to them and build a relationship. And children playing in your neighborhood can provide an excellent bridge for meeting their parents.

Visit the Field

As you begin to pray, read, and connect with internationals, you may find your relationships provide an invitation to visit a foreign country. If you've never traveled overseas, join an existing team or a seasoned traveler. If your church has a mission program get involved and volunteer for a short term mission trip. Some programs introduce women to women's programs in another country so they can build relationships.

Another way to be introduced to a nation is to join a prayer journey team and visit a country to pray on-sight. Christians living in the Muslim world have often remarked that after a prayer team has visited their city they find their Muslim neighbors more receptive to the gospel.

Today, God is moving in unprecedented ways all over the world. There is a ripe spiritual harvest in practically every country. All you have to do is have an open heart and mind and the Holy Spirit will show you the role He has for you.

A Story from the Field

Theresa was invited to visit a village in Kenya. As a board member of a U.S. organization that worked in developing countries in the Third World, she wanted to see the field firsthand. As a woman, she was eager to meet women from other cultures and see how they lived and worked. What she witnessed in the course of a few days changed her life.

Reading about the third world is one thing. Seeing it firsthand is another. As women from the village came to meet Theresa, she noticed that many of them had callused hands and severely curved spines. Daily they navigated a steep, 45-minute hike to the village well to fetch water for the day. This excursion wreaked havoc on the women's backs. In time, they experienced spinal injuries that limited their mobility for life. Seeing their condition Theresa was deeply moved in her spirit to do something.

"Is there another way to fetch the water?" Theresa asked.

The women were eager to talk. "Yes, we already have a solution." Their plan was to place water tanks on the rooftops of their homes and catch the rainwater. They could attach pipes to the tanks and access their water supply without carrying it on their backs. The plan would work, but the tanks were prohibitively expensive—about $2,500 each. Theresa pondered their predicament and said nothing.

Upon her return to the U.S. she went to visit relatives in Texas. Her burden for those Kenyan women was deep, and she could not stop talking about what she saw and heard. In just a few days, people began responding with donations. Theresa was ecstatic. *What if I shared this opportunity with more of my friends?* she thought. To her surprise each time she shared the story of the Kenyan women, people were moved to donate funds for the tanks. In a matter of months Theresa had raised enough money to purchase forty tanks. The project was underway.

All it took was one visit from a young single woman who had a heart big enough to tell the story and change the lives of women in Kenya. Theresa's ministry now helps women with small loans and training to build businesses that support their families.

Take time to learn what God is doing around the world. Expect Him to tug at your heart. When it happens, follow His leading. Small steps of faith build confidence for bigger steps. It's an adventure worth taking. Before you know it, your life will take on a new dimension, allowing you and the world to never be the same.

Developing Your Strategy
For Mission Involvement

Recently I had lunch with a highly successful media executive and her associate. Both were full of questions, eager to learn all about the different countries I had traveled and all that God was doing around the world. At one point in the conversation the two women looked at each other and said, "And what are we doing to make a difference?" There was an awkward pause but one that ended on a high note.

"You see, you don't have to travel the world to make a difference for the Lord," I replied. You can be a World Christian and learn to stand in the *Gap* between *God's world-wide purpose and its fulfillment."*

There is more than one kind of response to that Gap. Some World Christians stand in the Gap through prayer, particularly at its widest end where billions await the opportunity to hear of Christ for the first time. Others are willing to be broken and remolded to fit the Gap wherever they can make the most strategic impact. It may involve giving sacrificially or using their profession to open doors for ministry. Some World Christians choose to stand in the Gap by physically crossing major human barriers (cultural, political, spiritual) to bring the gospel to those who can hear no other way. Others write about it so other generations can become informed.

According to David Bryant, Founder of Concerts of Prayer International, a World Christian isn't better than other Christians. But by God's grace, they have made a discovery so important that life can never be the same again. They have discovered the truth about the Gap, and the call of Christ to believe, think, plan, and act accordingly. By faith, they have chosen to stand in the Gap as a result.[27]

If you aren't already involved in a mission activity take time to pray for a nation, especially one whose people have yet to hear the Gospel. As you pray, God will give you His heart and perspective on them and make you want to become their advocate. That's how you begin to know the truth about the Gap. In time the Lord will show you the unique role He wants you to play. That's how you find your place in the Gap and become a World Christian. It all begins with prayer and it changes you forever!

> *Rejoice with those saints, unpraised and unknown,*
> *Who bear someone's cross or shoulder their own.*
> *They shame our complaining, our comforts, our cares.*
> *What patience in caring, what courage is theirs.*
>
> *Some march with events to turn them to God's way,*
> *Some need to withdraw the better to pray.*
> *Some carry the gospel through fire and through flood,*
> *Our world is their parish their purpose is God.*
>   (Rejoice in God's Saints)

Read, Reflect, & Respond

Bible Study

Take a few minutes alone to read and reflect on the following Scripture. Record your thoughts in a journal.

> DANIEL 12:3. *And those who have insight will shine brightly like the brightness of the expanse of heaven, and those who lead the many to righteousness, like the stars, forever and ever.*

When was the last time you personally led someone to the Lord?

Homework Questions

We are most often consumed with the problems and challenges in our own lives. Take a spiritual sabbatical with the Lord—perhaps you could start with even 15 minutes. Ask Him to show you a nation or a people He wants you to pray for. Do some research and use that information to fuel your prayer for them.

Small Group Question

When there is a horrible tragedy in the world—a devastating earthquake, an outbreak of war, or a mass killing—what is your first response? How does God want you to respond? How have you responded in the past?

Recommended Reading

Beyond Duty, Tim Dearborn (MARC Publications: Monrovia, California). An excellent book about mission theology and God's heart for the world.

Operation World: The Day-to-Day Guide to Praying for the World, Patrick Johnstone, (Zondervan Publishing House: Grand Rapids, Michigan, 1998).

Prayer Walking, Steve Hawthorne and Graham Kendrick (Creation House: Orlando, Florida). Information on how to pray on-site with insight.

Strongholds of the 10/40 Window, edited by George Otis, Jr. with Mark Brockman (YWAM Publishing: Seattle, Washington). Intercessor's guide for praying for the world's least evangelized nations.

Where Does My Pathway Lead from Here?

Thank you for taking the time to read this book. Hopefully you've acquired a new perspective on how to find God's purpose for your life. Revisit your answers on the self-assessment questionnaire at the beginning of the book. Can you see how you have become more focused and purposeful since first completing that form? Where are you in the development of your vision? If you're still not sure, let me help you with your next step. And if you know your vision, that's great!

If You Are Seeking Your Purpose

Are you still wondering about your gifts and calling? Don't fret. God has ways of working things out. Just keep asking these four simple questions:

1. How is God working in my life? If you're not sure, keep asking. Don't worry, you'll get an answer.
2. What are God's priorities for my life this year? Write them down and review them regularly. They're easy to forget.
3. What is my passion, and how can I use it in a place of great need? This will help you discover your calling.
4. Who do I know who can mentor me in an area of personal growth? We all need to learn from others.

If you don't have all the answers, *don't* close the book and walk away. Make a commitment to yourself to ask those four questions every few months. You may be surprised at the progress you make as you continuously review them.

Even when you fail, you learn valuable lessons. Remember that the difference between greatness and mediocrity is often how you view your mistakes. God is working His purpose in your life even when you don't know it.

If You Know Your Purpose

It is an exciting time when you finally discover your purpose. You are like a mother holding her newborn baby in her arms. It's a moment of unspeakable joy, full of promise. And with the joy comes the responsibility to nurture and keep that vision alive.

Finding a good mentor is important. If you are having difficulty, do what my friend DeLoris did. She made a commitment to learn from every leader she met.

As you build on your purpose, keep in mind these three things:
1. You have much to do and much to learn. Pace yourself. Don't be tempted to move too fast.
2. Seek counsel and the advice of wise mentors to guide you.
3. Too many early mistakes may undermine your vision. Use the lessons from your mistakes to gain wisdom for the future.

If You Are Developing Your Purpose

Good for you! You now have a solid foundation of knowledge and experience. Be generous with what God has given you. Remember to honor those who have helped you get there. As your purpose continues to evolve and mature, look for ways to empower others who could benefit from your work. Walk them through the lessons you've learned.

Continue to be a good steward of your purpose and vision. Don't be tempted to compromise your standards or values. Your purpose may evolve, but it must always stay true to its original foundation. Success has a way of changing us in good and bad ways. The choice is ultimately yours. Keep in mind three things:

- Don't allow yourself to be defined by your successes (or your failures).
- Be generous with what God has given you. Look for ways to bless others.
- Don't compromise your standards or the stewardship of your vision.

And wherever you are in developing your vision and purpose, don't underestimate the power of networking. Seek ways to connect with people who can encourage you, give you new ideas, support you, and provide you with valuable introductions.

One Last Word . . .

Chariots of Fire is one of my favorite movies. It's the true story of Eric Liddell, a Scottish runner who risked becoming a national disgrace when he refused to run on Sunday at the 1924 Paris Olympic Games, thus disqualifying himself from the finals. Criticism turned to national acclaim when Eric entered and won a race for which he was completely untrained, finishing a full five meters ahead of the favorite. The faith that inspired his courageous stand caused him to announce at the height of his fame that he was leaving athletics to be a missionary to the land of his birth, China.

As a boy, Eric was often asked why he ran so much. His answer was, "God made me fast, and when I run I feel His pleasure!"

While still in his thirties Eric took his last bow from this world. I'm sure when he met his Maker he heard the words, "Well done, good and faithful servant." I think in every heart there is a longing to accomplish great and noble things. But small tasks, when done in love, are also great and noble. We each have an important role to play.

Have you found God's pleasure yet? Don't give up until you do. And remember the process is just as important as the goal. My prayer is that this book has helped you in that journey.

END NOTES

Introduction
1. *Letter from Ed Dayton* dated September 16, 1999.
2. *Developing the Leader within You* (Nelson Publishers: Nashville, 1993) p. 1.

The Power of a Dream
3. *The Articulate Executive* (McGraw-Hill: New York, 1996) p. Xi.
4. *Letter from Ed Dayton* dated September 16, 1999.

The Art of Mentoring
5. *A Working Woman's Guide to Joy*, compiled by Gwen Weising (A Day Brightener product from Garborge's: Bloomington, Minnesota).

Know Your Limits
6. *Developing the Leader within You,* John Maxwell (Nelson Publishers:Nashville, 1993) p.38.
7. *Adopted from How to Get Things Done* (National Press Publications, 1998) p.7.
8. Adopted from *How to Get Things Done* (National Press Publications, 1998) p.11.

Integrity
9. *The 21 Irrefutable Laws of Leadership*, John Maxwell, (Thomas Nelson Publishers: Nashville, 1998.) p. 27.
10. *Integrity in a World of Pretense,* Earl Palmer (InterVarsity Press: Downer's Grove, Illinois, 1992).
11. *Management, Tasks, Responsibilities and Practices,* Peter Drucker, (New York: Harper & Row, 1974)

A Call to Excellence
12. *Developing the Leader within You* (Nelson Publishers: Nashville, 1993) p.164.
13. *Developing the Leader within You* (Nelson Publishers: Nashville, 1993) P.177.
14. Quoted by Charles Nutter in *Vital Speeches of the Day*, March 1, 1996.

Developing People
15. *Developing the Leader within You*, John Maxwell (Nelson Publishers: Nashville, 1993) p. 113.
16. *Woman of Influence,* Pam Farrel (InterVarsity Press: Downers Grove, Illinois p.87.
17. *Caring Enough to Confront,* David Augsburg, (Augsburg Press: Lynnwood, Washington).
18. *Developing the Leader within You*, John Maxwell (Nelson Publishers: Nashville, 1993) p.124.
19. *Powerful Leadership Skills for Women* (National Press Publications, 1998) p.74.

Opposites Do Not Always Attract
20. 24 *Free Reports,* (The Insiders Money Club, 1998) p.50.
21. *The Prince*, Machiavelli (The Great Books Foundation: Chicago, 1955) p. 55

END NOTES

22. *Quotable Quotes,* (The Readers Digest, January 2000 issue)
23. *Powerful Leadership Skills for Women* (National Press Publications, 1998) p.37.
24. Strike it Rich, A Smart Way a Secretary Made Millions (Ladies Home Journal, June, 2000 issue)
25. *Developing the Leader within You,* John Maxwell (Nelson Publishers: Nashville, 1993) p.202.

Something to Die For
26. MARC newsletter, September 1993.
27. Worldwide Perspectives (William Carey Library, Pasadena, CA 1999) p.707.

TESTIMONIES FROM AROUND THE WORLD

Since its initial printing in 2000, this book has been read by women in over 20 nations including India, Bosnia, South Africa, Korea, Greece, Australia, Spain, Rumania, Switzerland, Germany, Brazil, China, Singapore and many others. This is an hour when God is calling women to step outside their comfort zone and follow Him in service to their community, their nation and the world. Here are quotes from some of the women touched by this book.

For the first time in years, I believe that some of my old dreams may still be a part of God's plan for me. Reading *Pathway to Purpose* caused me to evaluate my life and begin to dream again. I realize that the desires and dreams in my heart are God-given. I have been challenged to not take life as it comes my way but to make choices to aggressively pursue God's purpose and destiny for my life. I highly recommend this workbook. It will change the life of every women who reads it.

God showed me how to implement His principles in my business and it has grown beyond my expectations.

I now have a plan to unclutter and get organized, I also have some new goals.

At first I underestimated how God would use *Pathway to Purpose* to change my life. Now I know it is based on a great deal of prayer. I feel that I have been picked up, shaken around and re-arranged in ways that have helped me better understand myself and others.

Pathway to Purpose has helped me develop a deeper level of integrity - to understand the untruths we believe and in particular the masks we wear. That has had a big impact in my life that is richly rewarding. I feel I've changed a lot with the knowledge that is given in this book.

I've learned so much from *Pathway to Purpose* by studying it with other women. It gave me a sense of personal worth and self-esteem. I now feel challenged to live and walk in God's standards instead of comparing myself to others.

RE-ORDER AND FEEDBACK INFORMATION

Your feedback is important to the author. Please direct questions, comments, or additional orders of this book to:

Kathy Giske
PO Box 82672
Kenmore, WA 98028, USA

Phone: (425) 485-7237
E-mail: segiske@yahoo.com

Bulk order discounts apply.

Speaking engagements requests of the author can be directed at the above address.

For information on how to start a Women's Leadership Network Chapter in your community Email: WLNSEATTLE@aol.com